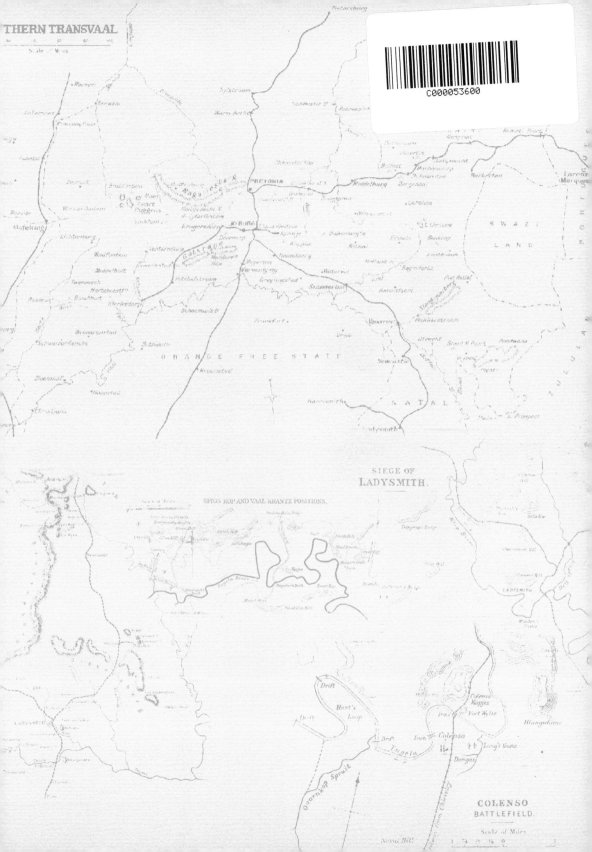

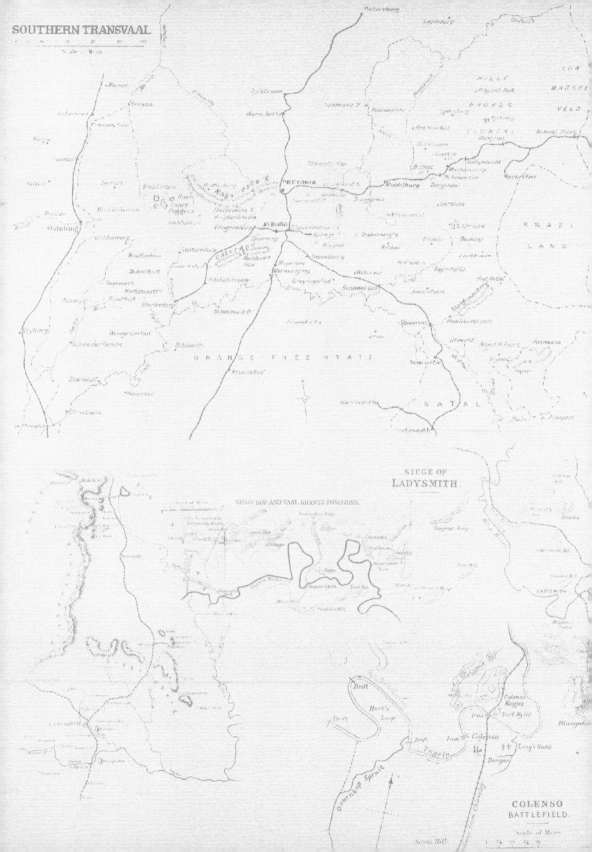

SOUTH AFRICA

Churchill's

SOUTH AFRICA

TRAVELS DURING THE ANGLO-BOER WAR

CHRIS SCHOEMAN

Published by Zebra Press
an imprint of Random House Struik (Pty) Ltd
Reg. No. 1966/003153/07
Wembley Square, First Floor, Solan Road, Gardens, Cape Town, 8001
PO Box 1144, Cape Town, 8000, South Africa

www.zebrapress.co.za

First published 2013

1 3 5 7 9 10 8 6 4 2

Publication © Zebra Press 2013
Text © Chris Schoeman 2013

Quotations from *Ian Hamilton's March* (1900), *London to Ladysmith via Pretoria* (1900)
and *My Early Life* (1930) reproduced with permission of Curtis Brown, London,
on behalf of the Estate of Sir Winston Churchill. Copyright © Winston S. Churchill

All rights reserved. No part of this publication may be reproduced,
stored in a retrieval system or transmitted, in any form or by any means,
electronic, mechanical, photocopying, recording or otherwise,
without the prior written permission of the copyright owners.

PUBLISHER: Marlene Fryer
MANAGING EDITOR: Robert Plummer
EDITOR: Mark Ronan
PROOFREADER: Bronwen Leak
COVER AND TEXT DESIGNER: Jacques Kaiser
TYPESETTER: Monique van den Berg
INDEXER: Sanet le Roux

Set in 10.5 pt on 14.5 pt Minion

Printed and bound by CTP Book Printers, Duminy Street, Parow, 7500

ISBN 978 1 92054 547 5 (print)
ISBN 978 1 77022 532 9 (ePub)
ISBN 978 1 77022 533 9 (PDF)

Contents

Introduction

WINSTON CHURCHILL WAS NOT ONLY a famous British statesman, but also a prolific author and historian. During his early years, his position as a war correspondent enabled him to experience adventures in India, the Sudan and South Africa, which he vividly described in books such as *The River War*, *London to Ladysmith via Pretoria*, *My African Journey* and *My Early Life*. In addition, Churchill wrote monumental works of history, which included *The World Crisis, 1916–1918* (on World War I), *The Second World War* and *A History of the English-Speaking Peoples*. In 1953 he received the Nobel Prize for Literature, as well as a knighthood.

Churchill pursued a military career not as an end in itself but as a stepping stone to a political career, and he used a two-pronged approach to achieve this, namely by creating hero worship around himself and through his writing. He had a reputation as someone who sought war medals, and he maintained a strict regime of reading and writing, even in sweltering Indian or African conditions. Like another famous English writer, Rudyard Kipling, Churchill covered the Anglo-Boer War as a newspaper correspondent. They worked for the *Friend of the Free State* and the *Morning Post*, respectively. In later years, both looked back on the war in their autobiographies. As well as several short stories on the subject, Kipling devoted a chapter of his autobiography, *Something of Myself*, to his war experience, while Churchill described his wartime adventures in *London to Ladysmith via Pretoria*, *Ian Hamilton's March* and *My Early Life*. But although both writers witnessed the war in fairly similar conditions, Churchill presented the Boers as loyal enemies, to be fought but respected, whereas Kipling viewed the Boers as treacherous guerrillas who deserved no mercy. Kipling took a violent dislike to individual politicians, and Churchill was one of them. But, ironically, Churchill was one of Kipling's great admirers.

It has been said that much of what Churchill wrote probably did not happen quite the way he conveyed it, and that there were events that only happened in his mind. There is a fine line between truth and imagination, and those not thoroughly familiar with the circumstances in South Africa at that time would hardly have been able to distinguish between fact and fiction, especially if they lived several thousand miles away. But all the blame for misrepresenting certain situations cannot be laid solely at Churchill's door. Often newspaper editors, biographers and historians unquestioningly accepted his writings as fact, and interpretations of events may even have been manipulated for the sake of dramatisation and glorification, and to suit individuals' personal views on certain issues.

Churchill himself has been accused of manipulation. In 1927, Major General Sir Frederick Maurice, in assessing Churchill's book *The World Crisis, 1916–1918* in *Foreign Affairs*, wrote:

Mr Churchill is a student of [historian/poet] Macaulay. Unfortunately he has confined his studies to the literary methods of the master ... We experience all the charm of novelty, we are swept along by the exuberance and compelling force of our author, and are little disposed to pause and question his facts.

This method, admirably suited to the politician on the platform, whose object is to persuade an audience not likely to be too well informed of detail, has its dangers when applied to the printed word, and particularly to the printed word dressed in the guise of history ... A public still appalled by the sacrifices of war is only too ready to listen to attacks upon those who called for those sacrifices. Mr Churchill supplies them with a full measure of those attacks. Almost every general, British, French and German, concerned in the war in the West is exhibited to us as a slow-witted, unimaginative blunderer who sent his men to useless slaughter.[1]

Churchill's ways in military and social circles, and his writings, which were aimed at accomplishing his political goals, made him popular with some but unpopular with others. It seems that in South Africa during the Anglo-Boer

War he was tolerated though disliked by British military commanders such as Sir Redvers Buller, Lord Roberts and Lord Kitchener. Soon after his arrival in the Cape, and while in the company of Buller and the governor of the Cape Colony, Churchill expressed his views on how the campaign should be run. Buller's reply was 'Don't be such a young ass'. And on another occasion, a group of colonels and generals sent him a telegram with the message: 'Best friends here hope you will not continue making further ass of yourself.'[2]

As we will see later in this book, Churchill also got on the wrong side of Roberts and Kitchener because of some journalistic comments he made. During a visit to Khartoum in 1907, which had been shelled by the British in the Battle of Omdurman in 1898, Churchill sent several memoranda back to the Colonial Office. A senior official, Sir Francis Hopwood, wrote to the colonial secretary, Lord Elgin: 'He is most tiresome to deal with and will I fear give trouble – as his father [Sir Randolph Churchill] did – in any position to which he may be called. The restless energy, uncontrollable desire for notoriety and the lack of moral perception make him an anxiety indeed.'[3] And the editor of the *North American Review*, William McRiderley, scribbled a note saying, 'Cheeky little cuss, ain't he?'

But some also recognised his potential as a politician and statesman. During the Siege of Ladysmith in the Anglo-Boer War, Sir George White was talking to a group of officers, when, according to an eyewitness, Churchill 'came up to the group; with a good deal of sang-froid and not much ceremony, he made his way through the group, and in a very audible voice at once engaged [White] in a short conversation, then went off'. Asked by one of the officers who the individual was, White replied, 'That's Randolph Churchill's son Winston; I don't like the fellow, but he'll be Prime Minister of England one day.'[4] In 1896, Captain Aylmer Haldane, a fellow officer of Churchill's in India, predicted that in ten years he would become leader of the House of Commons and by then or sooner, the secretary of state for India.

In his early years especially, Churchill tended to be melodramatic and boastful in his writings, as his letters and dispatches from the war front illustrate. After the cavalry charge of the 21st Lancers at the Battle of Omdurman in September 1898, for instance, he described to his mother (and mothers like to believe everything their sons tell them) how he had been under fire all day and miraculously escaped uninjured. 'I fired 10 shots with my pistol – all necessary – and just got to the end of it as we cleared the crush. I never felt the slightest nervousness and felt as cool as I do now … I am sorry to say I shot 5 men for certain and two doubtful … Nothing touched me. I destroyed those who molested me and so passed out without any disturbance of body or mind.'[5]

Hinting at his possible death in battle – perhaps also attributable to youthful melodrama – is a recurring theme in Churchill's letters during his African and Indian campaigns. On 28 January 1900, he wrote from Spioen Kop to Pamela Plowden: 'I do not know whether I shall see the end or not, but I am quite certain that I will not leave Africa until the matter is settled … My place is here: here I stay – perhaps forever.' He also mentions, 'I had five very dangerous days – continually under shell and rifle fire and once the feather in my hat was cut through by a bullet … I wonder whether we shall get through and whether I shall live to see the end … My nerves were never better and I think I care less for bullets every day.'[6]

There's the old adage 'never let the truth stand in the way of a good story' – one that the Churchill of the Anglo-Boer War years seemed to embrace when it suited his aspirations. He could write about his thrilling adventures so convincingly that few would doubt his daring exploits. South Africans familiar with the Pretoria environs still chuckle at Churchill's alleged statement that he 'swam the mighty Apies River' after his escape from prison, as the river in question is at best ankle deep. But although some claim that Churchill himself told the story during his lecture tour of the United States after his return from the war, he never mentioned it in his dispatches to London's *Morning Post* or in his autobiographies, *My Early Life* and *London to Ladysmith via Pretoria*, in which he wrote about his earlier adventures in South Africa. His escape from prison and journey through the Transvaal to Portuguese East Africa (Mozambique) were not considered by the British military – or the Boers, for that matter – to be great feats. But he was nevertheless hailed by the pro-British press as having pulled off one of the greatest military escapes on record. And through his dispatches and subsequent memoirs he literally and figuratively cashed in on the situation.

Winston Churchill was a marvellous storyteller and he knew how to keep his readers captivated. He had a wonderful command of the English language, and his descriptions of landscapes, places and events are vivid and lively. A fellow war correspondent, John Black Atkins of the *Manchester Guardian*, described him well: 'It was obvious that he was in love with words. He would hesitate sometimes before he chose one or would exchange one for a better … I had not encountered this sort of ambition, unabashed, frankly egotistical, communicating its excitement, and extorting sympathy.'[7]

Arguably his most exciting early work, *London to Ladysmith via Pretoria* (1900), describes Churchill's Boer War experiences, including his escape from the Boer prison in Pretoria and his return to British lines via Lourenço Marques (now Maputo, Mozambique). *Ian Hamilton's March* (1900), the sequel, and a book that contains some of his best writing on his early military campaigns, deals with the British marches on and occupation of Bloemfontein and Pretoria, and Churchill's re-entry into the Transvaal capital to help free his fellow prisoners from the same prison in which he had been incarcerated months before.

Though not entirely accurate in places, *My Early Life* (1930), which contains his war memoirs, is regarded as Churchill's most beloved and engaging work. In it he wrote, 'The wonderful air and climate of South Africa, the magnificent scale of its landscape, the life of unceasing movement and of continuous incident made an impression on my mind which even after a quarter of a century recurs with a sense of freshness and invigoration.'[8] It is these impressions that *Churchill's South Africa* aims to convey through Churchill's own words, supplementary sources and contemporary and present-day photographs. Although this book has as its background the Anglo-Boer War, it is not a military history book in the traditional sense, dominated by military leaders and detailed accounts of battles. Instead it focuses on Churchill's footsteps across South Africa and looks at the places he visited, the people he met and his interactions with them, and the variety of landscapes he encountered. Churchill traversed all four provinces of Victorian South Africa – the Cape Colony, Natal, Orange Free State and Transvaal (he even travelled as far as Komatipoort on the Mozambican border) – so the whole country is well represented in this account.

1

Early life and military career

'The Boer ultimatum had not ticked out on the tape machines
for an hour before Oliver Borthwick came to offer me an
appointment as principal War Correspondent of the Morning Post.
[£]250 a month, all expenses paid, entire discretion as to
movements and opinions, four months' minimum guarantee
of employment – such were the terms, higher, I think, than any
previously paid in British journalism to War Correspondents,
and certainly attractive to a young man of twenty-four with
no responsibilities but to earn his own living.'[1]

WINSTON LEONARD SPENCER CHURCHILL WAS born on 30
November 1874 at Blenheim Palace in Oxfordshire into a Victorian
aristocratic family as the eldest son of the prominent Tory MP, Lord Randolph Churchill, and American heiress Jennie Jerome. Blenheim, though,
was never Winston Churchill's 'home'. His father was the third son of the
seventh Duke of Marlborough, and lived in the palace from the age of eight
until he married. The estate eventually passed to his eldest brother, Winston's uncle.

Throughout the night of Winston's birth, the rain beat at the windows
and the wind ripped through the oak trees in the grounds – perhaps an omen
of the stormy and eventful life that lay ahead for the child. Dr Frederick
Taylor struggled all night to supervise the birth, which was difficult and painful, but at 1.30 on a Monday morning, Winston Churchill was brought into
the world.

He was born into the lap of luxury, and his parents were closely connected
with the influential political personalities of the day, which went a long way

Blenheim Palace, Oxfordshire, birthplace of Winston Churchill

to ensuring his swift promotion through the military ranks. Up to the time of the Anglo-Boer War, Churchill's adventures had much to do with his parentage and the influence his mother could exert upon his superiors.

When Churchill was a boy of four, Britain was fighting a war with the Zulus in South Africa. He recalled pictures in the British papers during the Zulu War of 1879, which portrayed the Zulus as black, naked and armed with assegais. As a child, his mind was stirred by Britain's colonial wars such as this one. From his early youth, Churchill brooded about soldiers and war, and would often try to envisage the sensation of being under enemy fire.

His early education was at a preparatory school in Brighton, where he was a pupil in the dancing class; a Miss Eva Moore taught the young Churchill the steps of the Lancers Quadrille. Her memory of him was that of a 'small, red-headed pupil, the naughtiest boy in the class; I used to think he was the naughtiest small boy in the world!'[2] Even some of his relatives were not too fond of him. The Duchess of Marlborough, Consuelo,[3] for instance, recalls in *The Glitter and the Gold* the following words that her mother, dowager Duchess Alva Erskine Smith, said to her: 'Your first duty is to have a child, and it must be a son, because it would be intolerable to have that little upstart Winston become a duke.'[4]

From prep school in Brighton, Churchill went to Harrow, where he met influential people like Leo Amery, the future well-known historian. Another important figure in the young Churchill's schooldays was Louis Moriarty, a beefy figure with a walrus moustache, and later his tutor in the army class.

Early life and military career | 7

Churchill as a young boy

Moriarty helped to develop Churchill's skills as a writer and instil in him his lifelong fascination with history. At Harrow, Churchill struggled through the classics and found that he wasn't particularly bright when it came to using a dictionary, didn't shape too well as a senior wrangler and was bottom of the class when he passed the preliminary examination for the army. In terms of sports, he took up riding, cricket, boxing and fencing, in which he won the Public School Championship. He believed that all his contemporaries seemed in every way better adapted to school life and were far superior both at games and academic work.

According to Aylmer Haldane, who later served as captain with Churchill during the Anglo-Boer War, Bishop Welldon, Churchill's headmaster at Harrow, recalled that

> he had birched him more frequently than any other boy, but with little effect. This obstreperous, irresponsible pupil had managed to express himself regarding the Head – I imagine in covert terms – in the school magazine; and he added to these interesting disclosures, to my amusement, that on one occasion Churchill had even had the audacity to tell him how to perform his duties.[5]

In 1941, having survived several colonial wars, World War I and the first years of World War II, Churchill would give a famous speech at his alma mater, in which he stressed that one should never give in, in anything one did.

James Tomlin, a head boy during Churchill's time at Harrow, recalled him as 'this small, red-haired, snub-nosed, jolly-faced youngster darting up during a house debate, against all the rules, before he had been a year in the house, to refute one of his seniors and carrying all before him with a magnificent speech'.[6]

After Harrow, Churchill went to the Royal Military Academy at Sandhurst, from where he graduated in 1894. Sandhurst is situated in lovely Surrey woodland near Camberley, with lakes for boating and swimming, football and cricket grounds, tennis courts, racquet courts, a golf course, a gymnasium, riding schools and stables, shooting ranges and parade grounds. It was home to 360 military cadets, subjected to much stricter discipline than they had been accustomed to at school.

On hearing of his son's successful admission to Sandhurst, his father wrote to him:

The first extremely discreditable feature of your performance was missing the infantry, for in that failure is demonstrated beyond refutation your slovenly happy-go-lucky harum scarum style of work for which you have always been distinguished at your different schools … With all the advantages you had, with all the abilities which you foolishly think yourself to possess and which some of your relations claim for you, with all the efforts that have been made to make your life easy and agreeable and your work neither oppressive or distasteful, this is the grand result that you come up among the 2nd rate and 3rd rate class who are only good for commissions in a cavalry regiment … I am certain that if you cannot prevent yourself from leading the idle useless unprofitable life you have had during your schooldays and later months, you will become a mere social waistrel, one of the hundreds of the public school failures, and you will degenerate into a shabby unhappy and futile existence.[7]

But Lord Randolph had struggles of his own. In need of finances, he sailed to South Africa in 1891 and travelled to Mashonaland, a northern region of what is now Zimbabwe, in search of wealth from gold, having formed a prospecting syndicate. In South Africa he was treated like royalty, and the well-known author, politician and mining financier Percy Fitzpatrick was specially asked by mining magnate Alfred Beit to lead the expedition. Lord Randolph's dreams of striking it rich in South Africa never materialised, however, and he only succeeded in antagonising the Boers, who he had predicted would 'pass away unhonoured, unlamented … handed down to posterity by tradition as having conferred no single benefit upon any single human being …'[8] As an amateur journalist, Randolph Churchill had been contracted to write for the *Daily Graphic*, where he described the Boers as dirty, lazy and uncivilised. So when his son Winston came to South Africa eight years later, these insults had not yet been forgotten or forgiven.

At Sandhurst, where the daily routine was digging trenches, building breastworks and revetting parapets with sandbags, the young Winston collected a small military library. His greatest pleasure, however, was horses, a passion that remained with him until late in his life. He achieved his best marks in tactics, fortifications and riding. In contrast with his schooldays, he made many friends at Sandhurst, but the Anglo-Boer War took the lives of a large number of them, as did the Great War of 1914–1918.

At the Aldershot army base in 1895, Churchill became one of the inner circle of officers. Those who could not afford to keep their own horses were unwelcome. One such man was Second Lieutenant Alan Bruce, whom Churchill and his friends allegedly conspired against, with the result that Bruce was expelled. But the event had unsavoury consequences for Churchill and his associates. The editor of society newspaper *Truth*, Henry du Pré Labouchere, stated in the House of Commons that he did not believe that 'a more disreputable set of young men existed in the whole army', and he reported on the

Churchill's father, Lord Randolph Churchill

incident in his paper.[9] But worse still, Bruce's father, Alan Bruce-Pryce, a respectable barrister, stated that Churchill's dislike of his son was because his son 'knew too much about Winston, particularly about the case of a Sandhurst cadet who had been flogged publicly by a subaltern for committing acts of gross immorality "of the Oscar Wilde type" with Churchill'.[10] Although Bruce-Pryce later had to withdraw his accusations, at the time of the Bruce incident Churchill had apparently admitted to young Canadian millionaire Max Aitken (later to become Lord Beaverbrook) that he had had a homosexual affair out of curiosity. Later reports also claimed that Churchill had engaged in homosexual activities, notably with Ivor Novello, an actor and composer. Churchill allegedly admitted to this relationship to the well-known playwright and novelist, Somerset Maugham.[11] Interestingly, Lord Randolph had been described by Lord Salisbury, the Conservative Party leader and later British prime minister, as having an 'essentially feminine' temperament, and never having 'been able to get on with women'.[12]

Churchill as an officer in the 4th Queen's Own Hussars

Winston's mother pulled powerful strings, as was her wont, and the scandal did not prevent him from pursuing his military career. In November 1895, soon after graduating, Churchill travelled to Cuba via New York to observe the Spanish Army, where he wrote vividly descriptive articles for the *Daily Graphic.* Then, in the spring of 1896, he set off with the 4th Hussars for India and the north-west frontier to report for the *Pioneer* and *Daily Telegraph.* There he encountered Haldane again, who wrote:

> I cannot recall exactly how long he remained with us ... The period, however, was quite long enough to allow one to form an opinion of the young cavalry officer who was widely regarded in the army as superprecocious, indeed by some as insufferably bumptious, and realise that neither of these epithets was applicable to him. On the contrary, my distinct recollection of him at this time was that he was modest and paid attention to what was said, not attempting to monopolise the conversation or thrust his opinions – and clear-cut opinions they were on many subjects – on his listeners. He enjoyed giving vent to his views on matters military and other, but there was nothing that could be called aggressive or self-assertive which could have aroused antagonism among the most sensitive of those with whom he was talking ...

Haldane also established during his conversations with Churchill that he 'had no intention of making the army his profession', and noted that he would follow a political career.[13]

Two years later, Churchill joined Kitchener's army in the Sudan, commissioned to write articles for the *Morning Post.* He took part in

Horatio Herbert Kitchener, whom Churchill blamed for atrocities in the Sudan

Churchill in Cairo, 1898

the famous cavalry charge at the Battle of Omdurman with the 21st Lancers, after which he wrote *The River War*. In letters to his mother, he blamed Kitchener – who had a reputation for brutality – for battle atrocities in which more than 100 Dervishes were butchered. Kitchener had instructed his aide-de-camp in the Sudan, Major James Watson, not to hand over any documents to Churchill, but Churchill sidestepped the problem by interviewing the major in person and was able to finish writing his book. During the Anglo-Boer War, not long afterwards, it transpired that Kitchener had been offended by some passages in *The River War*, which nearly put an end to Churchill's chances of being attached as correspondent to the British forces marching upon Bloemfontein and subsequently Pretoria.

Churchill made his first political speech in 1899 after he had returned to England from the Sudan, resigned his army commission in the same year and stood in a by-election as a Conservative candidate in Oldham, where he was narrowly defeated.

In the meantime, war clouds had been gathering over the Boer republics of South Africa. The discovery of diamonds in Kimberley in the Northern Cape in 1871 set off a frenetic diamond rush and there was a massive influx of foreigners to the borders of the Orange Free State Republic. Then, in 1886, gold was discovered in the Transvaal, which prompted new waves of immigrants (who became known as Uitlanders) to rush to the Witwatersrand in search of fortune. The majority of these foreigners were from Britain and their numbers continued to grow until eventually the Uitlander population in the Transvaal exceeded that of the Boers. Lengthy negotiations took place between President Paul Kruger of the Transvaal and the British to reach a compromise on the Uitlanders' rights, but it didn't take Kruger long to realise that what was really at stake for the British was their ultimate control of the gold-mining industry. Key British colonial leaders, including Sir Alfred Milner, governor of the Cape Colony, the former Cape Colony prime minister, Cecil John Rhodes, the British colonial secretary, Joseph Chamberlain, and mining syndicate owners, such as Sir Alfred Beit, Barney Barnato and Lionel Phillips, favoured the annexation of the Trans-

vaal and Orange Free State. Confident that the two republics would be quickly defeated by the might of the British Army, they planned on a short war, which they thought would be over by Christmas 1899.

In September 1899, Joseph Chamberlain sent an ultimatum to President Kruger demanding full equality for the Uitlanders living in the Transvaal. In return, Kruger, who saw no other option than war, issued his own ultimatum, which stated that the British had forty-eight hours to withdraw all their troops from the border of the Transvaal. Failing that, the Transvaal and Orange Free State (which had an agreement of allegiance to the Transvaal in the event of war) would take up arms against the British in South Africa. Chamberlain rejected Kruger's ultimatum, and as a result the Transvaal declared a state of war with Britain.

A few months earlier, on 2 June

A British Boer War cartoon by artist Charles K. Cook. John Bull, in the guise of a British naval Tar, is in for a bit of a rude surprise from the seemingly harmless little Boer

Distributing Boer arms at the field cornet's office, Church Square, Pretoria, 11 October 1899

1899, Churchill had had breakfast with Cecil John Rhodes at the Burlington Hotel in London, where they discussed the growing crisis in the Transvaal. Rhodes was certain that war was now imminent, and after their conversation Churchill fully agreed.

Hardly had the news of the Boer ultimatum been broadcast than Oliver Borthwick of the *Morning Post* offered Churchill an appointment as the paper's chief war correspondent at £250 a month, with all expenses paid and four months' minimum guarantee of employment. To a young man of twenty-four, with a flair for adventure, it was a proposition of a lifetime. Churchill boarded the first steamer, the Royal Mail's *Dunnottar Castle*, on 14 October 1899, for South Africa. (Churchill gives his date of departure as

11 October, but correspondence dates and shipping records show that he boarded on the 14th, three days after the ultimatum had expired.)

Preparations occupied most of Churchill's time before his departure while London was abuzz with patriotic excitement and party controversy. News arrived that the Boers had taken the initiative and that their forces were advancing towards both the Cape Colony and Natal, that General Sir Redvers Buller had become the British commander-in-chief, that the reserves had been called out, and that the only army corps available was to be sent at once to Cape Town.

There was popular enthusiastic support for Buller, the Ashanti and Zulu Wars veteran, who many of the British people believed would finish the war with the Boers before Christmas. This was a gross misconception, as the war dragged on until 31 May 1902. And, as

General Redvers Buller, first commander of the British forces in the Boer War

Churchill remarked in *My Early Life*, there would not be a war if the other man did not think he also had a chance. At the docks there was a large cheering crowd singing 'God Save the Queen' and, as the *Dunnottar Castle* steamed away, 'Rule Britannia'.

Although he would later be scathing of soldiers indulging in luxury at the war front, Churchill made sure he was quite comfortable himself. He took along an Indian soldier's valet, Thomas Walden, who had accompanied Lord Randolph to Mashonaland eight years before, and was therefore familiar with southern African conditions. Also aboard was Churchill's supply of drinks, consisting of a number of cases of champagne, port, whisky and vermouth.

British soldiers packing for the front at the Cape Town docks

In his pocket he had a most important letter of introduction and recommendation from Lord Chamberlain to Sir Alfred Milner, declaring him 'a very clever young fellow', with a 'reputation of being bumptious, but I have not myself found him so ...'[14] Other letters of introduction to rich and successful people in Cape Town included those from Alfred Beit, a man who made an enormous fortune from South African gold and diamonds.

Churchill was seriously considering producing a documentary film on the war in South Africa, which was to be a joint venture between himself and Murray Guthrie, a member of Parliament and distant relative of his. In correspondence, Churchill refers to the 'cinematograph scheme' and that it would require not more than £700 – each would pay half the expenses. They had to make all the arrangements and he would do all that was necessary in South Africa. While travelling to Southampton, from where he was to sail for Cape Town, Churchill wrote to Guthrie that he had noticed that the American Biograph Company had already sent out a moving-picture camera, and that he had no doubt that he could obtain very special pictures. His only fear was that all the theatres would be contracted to the American film company. The proposed venture did not materialise, but there is little doubt that, with his marvellous imagination, Churchill could well have been capable of producing something insightful and interesting on the war.

Unfortunately for Churchill, he was to miss the publication of his new book, *The River War*, launched in the first week of November 1899. He had recorded his six weeks' service in the Sudan under Kitchener in a remarkable 1000-page opus of two volumes. The book was both lauded and criticised, but the important thing was that it created publicity for the ambitious young man.

2

Across the Great Karoo

*'The sun is warm, and the air keen and delicious. But the scenery
would depress the most buoyant spirits. We climbed up the
mountains during the night, and with the daylight the train was
in the middle of the Great Karroo [sic]. Wherefore was this
miserable land of stone and scrub created? Huge mounds of
crumbling rock, fashioned by the rains into the most curious and
unexpected shapes, rise from the gloomy desert of the plain.'*[1]

WINSTON WAS NOT THE FIRST of the Churchill family to arrive in
South Africa at the time of the Boer War. When he sailed for Africa
on 14 October 1899, the Boers' siege of Mafeking had only started the day
before, but his aunt Lady Sarah Wilson, an elegant, handsome woman and
the wife of Captain Gordon Wilson, who was aide-de-camp to Lord Baden-
Powell, had already been in Mafeking with her husband since September.
Before and during the siege, Sarah Wilson was a correspondent for the British
Daily Mail. After receiving news of the Boer ultimatum of 11 October, Baden-
Powell ordered her to move to the nearby town of Setlagole, forty-six miles
south of Mafeking, but she soon went to the village of Mosita. There she
started passing on information to the British forces in Mafeking, but the
Boers became wise to her activities and she was put under house arrest. She
was later released in exchange for a spy and convicted horse thief by the
name of Petrus Viljoen,[2] and returned to Mafeking, where she was treated as
a heroine. She then excelled herself caring for the wounded, ill and homeless
while still working as a war correspondent.

At the end of the war, Sarah Wilson was probably the most celebrated
woman in Britain. But Winston Churchill and his aunt did not get along.

This may have been because of professional jealousy, but he doesn't mention her anywhere in his writings.

Along with Churchill, the *Dunnottar Castle* had on board the British Army commander, Sir Redvers Buller. When Buller's party had left London, rumours of battles and disasters were coming thick and fast, and were difficult to confirm or deny. It was only on the journey that they would learn of the Battle of Talana Hill in Natal and the death of Major General Penn Symons, the British commander in Natal, who was mortally wounded in the battle.

Four days after their departure, they reached the Portuguese island of Madeira, today just a three-and-a-half-hour flight from London. Passengers were hoping for news from the war, but learnt nothing. The correspondents were confronted with all kinds of speculation, ranging from fore-

Lady Sarah Wilson, Churchill's aunt. The two never got along

casts of the surrender of Pretoria to the British to the capture of the Cape by the Boer forces. On 23 October, they caught up with the *Nineveh*, a hired carrier transporting the Australian Lancers to the Cape. Signals were exchanged, and the Australians asked whether Sir Redvers Buller was on board. When they learnt that he was, the lancers gave three cheers and waved their broad-brimmed hats. But soon the speed of the *Dunnottar Castle* told, and she left behind the *Nineveh*. Six days later, they passed a large homeward-bound steamer by barely 200 yards, whose crew displayed a large board bearing a message in white paint: 'Boers defeated; three battles; Penn Symons killed.' The Battle of Talana Hill, at which Major General Penn Symons was killed on 20 October, was the first major clash of the Boer War. A frontal attack by British infantry supported by artillery drove Boers from their hilltop position, but the British suffered heavy casualties in the process.

The long sea voyage from England to the Cape came to an end when, on the afternoon of 30 October 1899, they sighted land; and soon they could make out the flat profile of Robben Island, then a barren piece of land inhabited by lepers and prisoners, but later to become world-famous as Nelson Mandela's place of captivity. With darkness descending, the ship entered Table Bay and by ten o'clock had reached the anchorage. In the distance, the lights of the city streets and houses gleamed brightly.

The *Dunnottar Castle* berthed alongside the quay and people with dispatches stepped on board, pushing through the crowd to General Buller's cabin. The war correspondents cornered what was presumably a passage agent to update them on developments on the war front. For the first time, Churchill and his colleagues learnt of the Battle of Talana Hill and the British casualties. They were also told of the battles of Elandslaagte (21 October), decisively won by the British, and Rietfontein (24 October), where General George White had pressed forward down the railway line from Glencoe to Ladysmith. In the Siege of Mafeking, according to one storyteller, 2000 Boers had been killed. This was quite an exaggeration, and not for a minute believed by Churchill.

British troops in Ladysmith, 30 October 1899

Table Mountain towering over Cape Town

Another English war correspondent, George Warrington Stevens, had arrived before Churchill, and described the city of Cape Town on 10 October, a day before the outbreak of war:

> Right in front rose three purple-brown mountains – the two supporters [Devil's Peak and Lion's Head] peaked, and Table Mountain flat in the centre. More like a coffin than a table, sheer steep and dead flat … exactly as he is in pictures; and as I gazed, I saw his tablecloth of white cloud gather and hang on his brow.
>
> The white line of houses nestling hardly visible between his foot and the sea must indeed be Capetown … The broad streets fronted with new-looking, ornate buildings of irregular heights and fronts were Western America; the battle of warming sun with the stabbing morning cold was Northern India. The handsome, blood-like electric cars, with their impatient gongs and racing trolleys, were pure

Cape Town docks during the Boer War

America … The niggers are very good-humoured, like the darkies of America. The Dutch tongue sounds like German spoken by people who will not take the trouble to finish pronouncing it. All in all, Capetown gives you the idea of being neither very rich nor very poor, neither over-industrious nor over-lazy, decently successful, reasonably happy, whole-heartedly easy-going.[3]

The war had altered Cape Town 'almost beyond recognition' according to Churchill's aunt, Lady Sarah Wilson, who had visited the city in 1895 before returning at the end of the Anglo-Boer War: 'From the dull and uninteresting seaport town … it seemed, seven years later, one of the busiest cities imaginable, with the most enormous street traffic. The pavements were thronged, the shops were crowded, and numerous were the smart, khaki-clad figures, bronzed and bearded, that were to be seen on all sides.'[4]

The centre of Cape Town as Churchill found it in 1899

The first prime minister of the Cape Colony, Sir John Molteno, wrote: 'There was life in those days ... The whole of the wealth of South Africa and much of the wealth of Great Britain was at home in the seaports ... The loyalists were the happiest, maddest and gayest people on the earth. Cape Town was the centre of the universe, not only the richest town of the Empire, but the most fashionable.'[5]

The morning after the *Dunnottar Castle* had docked, Buller landed in state and his arrival 'evoked one of the most striking popular demonstrations ever seen at Cape Town,' according to a *Times* correspondent. The ship was decked out in bunting from end to end, while a guard of honour of the Duke of Edinburgh's Volunteers lined the quay, where a huge crowd had gathered outside the docks. Amidst waving flags and cheering crowds, Buller was driven away in a carriage to Government House, a Georgian-style building typical of the period with a ballroom, a magnificent staircase and grand fireplaces.

(In 1968, the building was restored to its pre-1806 Dutch character, and is now known as Tuynhuys.)

The British officers, Churchill and other correspondents stayed at the well-known Mount Nelson Hotel, an excellent establishment where many of the leading Uitlanders took up accommodation during the war and hence its nickname, 'The Helot's Rest'. The hotel was completed in 1899, not long before the war, and was very popular with aristocrats and socialites drawn to South Africa by the excitement of the time. One of the historic landmarks of Cape Town, the hotel is set in a lush garden estate, as it was in Churchill's days, and is renowned for old-school glamour and luxury, and is a regular abode for international celebrities.

In a war letter, Captain B.J. Jones of the 1st Leinster Regiment sarcastically referred to the fashionable people who inhabited the hotel as the 'Mount Nelson garrison'. He also mentioned that 'the male part of the "garrison" are not supposed to be very eager for a life of outpost duty and quarter rations up country'.[6] The newly appointed resident commissioner for Bechuanaland (now Botswana), Sir Ralph Williams, wrote: 'Of all wonderful sights, the famous Mount Nelson Hotel was one of the most strange, packed as it was

The Mount Nelson Hotel, Cape Town, 1899

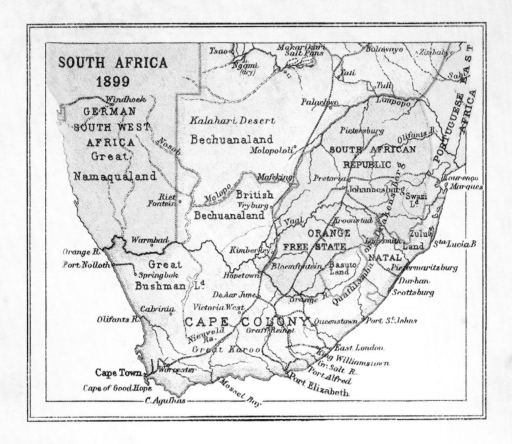

with officers from the front and their wives and friends, a medley of people, distinguished and undistinguished, all interested in one subject only, the war.'[7]

Churchill rather optimistically reckoned that there would be time for him to watch the British operations in Natal and then return to the Cape Colony to be part of the main British advance. Hoping to reach East London, from where he could board a small ship carrying the weekly English mail to Durban, Churchill packed his luggage at the Mount Nelson and left Cape Town by rail on the night of 31 October. He was accompanied by John Black Atkins of the *Manchester Guardian* and Captain Campbell of the Laffans Agency. From Durban, they were to continue to Ladysmith, a town that had been besieged by the Boers since 30 October. Other war correspondents were to sail from Cape Town to Durban on the *Dunnottar Castle* three days later. In the Orange Free

State, where the Boers were in control, all rail traffic had been interrupted, and to reach Natal by train Churchill and his companions had to travel 700 miles via De Aar Junction and Stormberg in the Northern Cape to East London, and from there by mailboat to Durban. There were concerns, however, that the train journey might be interrupted, as the railway line from De Aar Junction to Stormberg and Molteno ran parallel to the southern frontier of the Orange Free State, and Boer attacks were a possibility – even though none had been attempted in that area at that stage.[8]

On board the train, Churchill wrote to his mother that the British had greatly underestimated the military strength and fighting spirit of the Boers, and that he was expecting a fierce struggle in which thousands of lives were to be sacrificed. Among the Boers there was no doubt that they would emerge as the victors.[9]

The railway from the Cape to the north of the country passes through the historic Boland towns of Wellington (named after the Duke of Wellington and founded in 1840) and Worcester (founded in 1822), and through the Hex River Valley beyond, before the landscape opens up into the Great Karoo. Today, the most southernly defence relic of the Boer War – a multi-storey masonry blockhouse – still stands outside Wellington, but when Churchill passed through it had not yet been built. It was only in early 1901, when masonry blockhouses started to appear along the Wellington to Richmond section of this railway line, that eighteen of these blockhouses were erected to protect the main railway bridges. The town of Worcester still boasts a large number of historic Cape Dutch houses, all proclaimed national monuments. Its other claim to fame is that it was also the boyhood home of the winner of the 2003 Nobel Prize in Literature, John Maxwell Coetzee, author of *Disgrace*.

Beyond the Hex River Valley lies the Great Karoo, a vast, arid land characterised by hardy shrub and low, stony hills scattered here and there, and where temperatures in summer exceed thirty degrees Celsius. The first Karoo town Churchill came to was Touws River, still a small town today; then came the delightful village of Matjiesfontein, followed by Laingsburg, Beaufort West and De Aar. The latter was a large railway junction in the Northern Cape, which also served as an important British military depot. Trains going further

A typical Karoo landscape (near Three Sisters), that prompted Churchill to write, 'Wherefore was this miserable land of stone and scrub created?'

north crossed the Orange River and chugged through the diamond capital of Kimberley, then on to Johannesburg and Pretoria.

Churchill was quite content with his mode of travel. He found the train just as comfortable as those he had experienced in India, if more expensive, but the hardy Karoo landscape revealed itself in stark contrast to the green British Isles of his homeland:

> Lying-down accommodation is provided for all, and meals can be obtained at convenient stopping places. The train, which is built on the corridor system, runs smoothly over the rails – so smoothly, indeed, that I found no difficulty in writing. The sun is warm, and the air keen and delicious. But the scenery would depress the most buoyant spirits. We climbed up the mountains during the night, and with the daylight the train was in the middle of the Great Karroo [*sic*]. Wherefore was this miserable land of stone and scrub created? Huge mounds of crumbling rock, fashioned by the rains into the

most curious and unexpected shapes, rise from the gloomy desert of the plain. Yet, though the Karroo looks a hopeless wilderness, flocks of sheep at distant intervals – one sheep requires six hundred acres of this scrappy pasture for nourishment – manage to subsist; and in consequence, now and again the traveller sees some far-off farm.[10]

By contrast, war corrrespondent George Warrington Stevens recorded:

It is only to the eye that cannot do without green that the Karroo is unbeautiful. Every other colour meets others in harmony – tawny sand, silver-grey scrub, crimson-tufted flowers like heather, black ribs of rock, puce shoots of screes, violet mountains in the middle distance, blue fairy battlements guarding the horizon. And above all broods the intense purity of the South African azure – not a coloured thing, like the plants and the hills, but sheer colour existing by and for itself.

It is sheer witching desert for five hundred miles, and for aught I know five hundred miles after that. At the rare stations you see perhaps one corrugated-iron store, perhaps a score of little stone houses with a couple of churches. The land carries little enough stock – here a dozen goats browsing on the withered sticks goats love, there a dozen ostriches, high-stepping, supercilious heads in air, wheeling like a troop of cavalry and trotting out of the stink of that beastly train. Of men, nothing – only here at the bridge a couple of tents, there at the culvert a black man, grotesque in sombrero and patched trousers, loafing, hands in pockets, lazy pipe in mouth.[11]

Noticeboards at the railway stations along the route were placarded with Governor Alfred Lord Milner's proclamation against treason in the Cape Colony, printed in both English and Dutch. The Cape Colony belonged to the British Empire and, as such, its inhabitants were British subjects. Milner's proclamation warned subjects of their duties and responsibilities towards the Crown during this time of war.

One of the towns on the route was Matjiesfontein. Although Churchill mentions the place only in passing in *London to Lady-smith* (he writes that beyond Matjiesfontein every bridge and culvert was watched by a black with a flag to warn against unexpected demolitions), and not at all in *My Early Life*, Matjiesfontein would have delighted his writer's instincts. During the war, ex-trooper and war correspondent Edgar Wallace used the Matjiesfontein post office's brass telegraph to send his dispatches. And at the edge of the small village lay a large British remount camp, with over 20 000 horses and 10 000 soldiers stationed in the veld.

Edgar Wallace, the Boer War correspondent who became famous for his crime stories

To this day, Matjiesfontein has preserved its Victorian village charm. When a young immigrant Scot, James Logan, purchased land at 'Matjesfontein' (reeds fountain) in 1884, it was an insignificant railway halt in the depths of the Karoo. Logan made his money at the station by selling water to the railways for their locomotives and food to the train passengers. He then bought the land at Matjiesfontein and developed it into a prosperous village with a hotel, bank and post office. The Lord Milner Hotel, which was completed in 1899 before the outbreak of the Anglo-Boer War, served as headquarters of the Cape Western Command, and the village also supported a base hospital, with five of Logan's villas serving as convalescent homes for soldiers. By then, Matjiesfontein had become a fashionable watering place for weary travellers and those seeking relief for chest complaints in the clean, dry air.

Among Logan's distinguished visitors were Winston's father, Lord Randolph Churchill (still remembered there for borrowing a hunting dog that he never returned), Olive Schreiner, the famous author of several books, including *The Story of an African Farm*, who lived there for five years in her own cottage, and Rudyard Kipling, also a newspaper correspondent during the war and who made a special journey to visit Schreiner. In *The Native-Born*, Kipling writes about 'the smell of the baked Karoo'. And virtually all the British Army commanders, Lord Roberts, Douglas Haig and Edmund Ironside, stayed there. In the cemetery, to the west of the village, lies the grave

The Matjiesfontein train station

Matjiesfontein, *circa* 1900

The Lord Milner Hotel, Matjiesfontein

The Matjiesfontein graveyard, where some
notable figures are buried

British troops entering Beaufort West

of Major General Andy Wauchope, commander of the Highland Brigade, who was killed at the Battle of Magersfontein and whose widow gave Logan permission to have the Scottish general buried there.

Some 140 miles beyond this quaint little village, at Beaufort West, Churchill and his companions received news of the capitulation of 1 200 British soldiers near Ladysmith. Beaufort West had grown from a dusty village established on Hooyvlakte (hay flats) Farm in 1818 at the request of Lord Charles Somerset, governor of the Cape. Around 1900, the Karoo was teeming with entrepreneurs despite the war, and businessmen had sufficient confidence in the economy of the hinterland to launch new ventures and carry large stocks of supplies. Local newspapers of the day ran advertisements announcing seasonal sales and the arrival of large new stocks of items for purchase.[12] Beaufort West was the home town of the world-famous heart surgeon, Christiaan Barnard, to whom a museum has been dedicated there.

When Churchill reached De Aar, it had become clear that they were now much closer to the south-western battle front. Infantry and artillery detachments occupied the towns in the area, armoured trains were patrolling the line and small parties of armed police were guarding the bridges and culverts. The

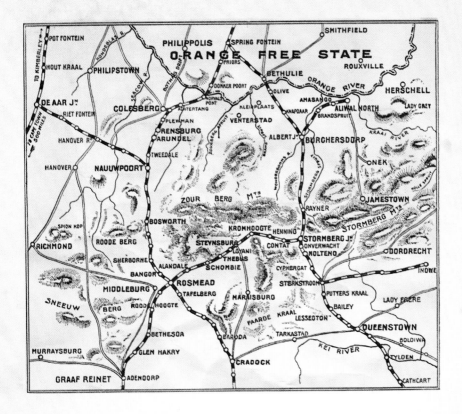

towns of De Aar, Naauwpoort, Arundel, Colesberg, Aliwal North, Norval's
Pont and Stormberg Junction were garrisoned with the limited number of
troops available at the time, and there were reports of Boer movements indi-
cating their imminent advance. The Boers had seized the bridge at Norval's
Pont across the Orange River and had cut the railway line between Bethulie
and Colesberg. Under the circumstances, the feeling was that each train that
left De Aar for Stormberg Junction could well have been the last to pass
through unscathed. 'De Aar is chiefly impressed on our minds by the heat,
dust, and flies,' recorded Captain Stratford St Leger of the mounted infantry
of General French's 1st Cavalry Brigade. He continues:

> In the pitiless, bare, and parched veldt a railway station, a church, and
> a few small houses have been planted, without shade or shelter of any

A young Tommy on the vast Karoo veld

kind, with the exception of a few blue gums which have grown up with the buildings. Several isolated ironstone koppies covered with stunted bush are dotted about to the east, south, and west of this uninviting spot.[13]

According to St Leger, only occasional patrols to Philipstown, an expedition to Prieska and guarding the Hanover Road railway bridge – where at least they had a river to bathe in – broke the monotony of being at De Aar.[14] For Churchill, the place would again have accentuated the vast contrast between his homeland and the barren Karoo.

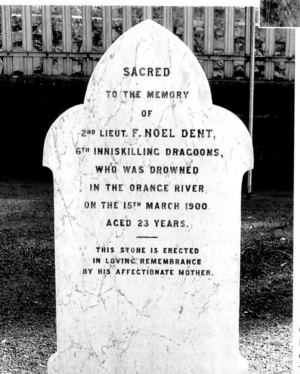

Colesberg seen from Coleskop, onto which the British managed to drag two 15-pounder guns. In the distance are the hills along the Orange River

Remains of an old Boer breastwork in the hills above Colesberg

SACRED
TO THE MEMORY
OF
2ND LIEUT. F. NOEL DENT,
6TH INNISKILLING DRAGOONS,
WHO WAS DROWNED
IN THE ORANGE RIVER.
ON THE 15TH MARCH 1900.
AGED 23 YEARS.
———
THIS STONE IS ERECTED
IN LOVING REMEMBRANCE
BY HIS AFFECTIONATE MOTHER.

Gravestone of 2nd Lieutenant Noel Dent, who drowned in the Orange River in March 1900. This is one of many graves in the Colesberg military cemetery

In the company of J.B. Atkins, the correspondent of the *Manchester Guardian* and later editor of *The Spectator*, Churchill started out for Stormberg. Their train was the last to get through, and when it reached Stormberg, the station staff were already packing up. Lying below a high hill called Rooikop, Stormberg Junction was situated along a wide expanse of rolling grass country, with rocky koppies on all sides. 'The wind screams down from the naked hills on to the little junction station,' wrote English correspondent George Stevens at the time (who died soon after of enteric fever). 'A platform with dining-room and telegraph office, a few corrugated-iron sheds, the station master's corrugated-iron bungalow – and there is nothing else of Stormberg but veldt and kopje, wind and sky ...'[15] And at times the area was struck by such severe thunderstorms that the thunder and lightning were frightening to those unaccustomed to it.

At Stormberg, Churchill and Atkins found confirmation of the rumour of a Boer advance on Burghersdorp, twenty-five miles away. When their train arrived, the evacuation of Stormberg by the British garrison was already under way. By then, the troops had been working night and day for more than a week to defend the junction; small redoubts were built on the koppies, entrenchments dug and the few houses near the station strongly fortified. But the garrison of twenty-five men was ordered to evacuate and retreat. Trains carrying the naval detachment, its guns and the Berkshires left, while the mounted infantry were already on the march. As they waited, an armoured train returned from patrolling and reported to have seen nothing of the advancing Boers. Waiting on the platform to go back to East London were also fifty Uitlanders from Johannesburg, who had been employed to make trenches. Their train finally left Stormberg Junction, and at Molteno, with its low, sandstone-built station, Churchill had a look around. Here about a hundred volunteers for the British cause got on board, as they too had been ordered to fall back. A correspondent of *The Times* mentioned that Churchill stayed at the Central Hotel in Molteno.[16]

Churchill provides no detail about his trip from Molteno to East London (although he did so on a return trip, as will be seen in a later chapter), which was some 170 miles to the south-east. They continued past Sterkstroom, through the vast landscape of open grassland dotted with aloes and rocky

The British evacuation of Stormberg

British troops entering Stormberg Junction

View of Molteno in 1899

The main street of Queenstown, *circa* 1900

Eastern Cape landscape, Amatola Mountains region

slopes, and on to the old British settler towns of Queenstown and Cathcart. Queenstown was a typical Eastern Cape settler town, predominantly English in appearance and ways. The small town of Cathcart, set in the foothills of the Amatola Mountains, originated from the British military post established in 1850 at Windvogelberg, in the division of Queenstown. Although the site was chosen primarily for its defensive potential, a number of civilians soon settled in its vicinity, and in 1876 it was named after Cape governor Sir George Cathcart. They were now travelling through what was then known as Tembuland, a region of grassy hills that had been populated by black tribes since the previous century – the land of Nelson Mandela's childhood. (Mandela was born in the winter of 1918 in the little village of Mvezo on the Mbashe River, near Umtata.) Churchill finally reached East London, South Africa's only river port, where the Buffalo River flows into the sea.

3

The green hills of Natal

*'The country between Estcourt and Colenso is open, undulating,
and grassy. The stations, which occur every four or five miles, are
hamlets consisting of half a dozen corrugated iron houses, and
perhaps a score of blue gum trees. These little specks of habitation
are almost the only marked feature of the landscape, which on
all sides spreads in pleasant but monotonous slopes of green.'[1]*

ORIGINALLY KNOWN AS PORT REX, East London was used as a supply
port to service the British military headquarters at King William's
Town, about thirty miles away. The town later developed into a settlement
of permanent residents, including Germans, which accounts for the names of
a number of towns in the vicinity, such as Stutterheim and Berlin. Today
German surnames are still common in the area, but the descendants of the
German settlers rapidly became anglicised.

When the war threatened, trainloads of Uitlander refugees arrived in East
London, some 5 000 of them, more than doubling the port's population within
a few months. Most of these had to rely on the goodwill of the residents
and lived in poor conditions in a tent town on Eastern Beach. But many East
London traders made a fortune from the war.

Aboard the steamer the *Umzimvubu*, Churchill sailed from East London
on 3 November into a fierce gale that caused huge waves and sent the little
ship rolling violently not far off the rugged Zululand shore. As could be
expected under these conditions, Churchill suffered terrible seasickness. He
was lying in a bunk in a stuffy cabin below deck at the stern of the ship,
and his misery continued through the afternoon, evening and night. It was
a voyage he was not likely ever to forget.

East London Harbour during the Boer War

The journey was delayed by some twenty hours because of headwinds.
It was only once they had passed Port St John's that the gale turned south-
west and added to their speed. As the heavy swell abated to some degree,
Churchill got the chance to take in the beauty of the coastline, nowadays
known in tourism circles as the Hibiscus Coast:

I had an opportunity of gaining some impressions of the general
aspect of the coasts of Pondoland and Natal. These beautiful
countries stretch down to the ocean in smooth slopes of the richest
verdure, broken only at intervals by lofty bluffs crowned with forests.
The many rivulets to which the pasture owes its life and the land its
richness glide to the shore through deep-set creeks and chines, or
plunge over the cliffs in cascades which the strong winds scatter into
clouds of spray.
　　These are regions of possibility, and as we drove along before our

The Natal South Coast

now friendly wind I could not but speculate on the future. Here are wide tracts of fertile soil watered by abundant rains. The temperate sun warms the life within the soil. The cooling breeze refreshes the inhabitant. The delicious climate stimulates the vigour of the European. The highway of the sea awaits the produce of his labour. All Nature smiles, and here at last is a land where white men may rule and prosper. As yet only the indolent Kaffir enjoys its bounty, and, according to the antiquated philosophy of Liberalism, it is to such that it should for ever belong. But while Englishmen choke and fester in crowded cities, while thousands of babies are born every month who are never to have a fair chance in life, there will be those who will dream another dream of a brave system of State-aided – almost State-compelled – emigration, a scheme of old-age pensions that shall anticipate old age, and by preventing paupers terminate itself;

a system that shall remove the excess of the old land to provide the deficiency of the new, and shall offer even to the most unfortunate citizen of the Empire fresh air and open opportunity.[2]

The small steamer reached Durban at midnight on 4 November. One of the few natural harbours along the southern African east coast, Durban dates back to around 1840, when the port was opened and became an extremely busy facility for ship repairs. At the time of Churchill's visit, the total population of the town was about 55 700, of whom 14 600 were black Africans. Today, the Port of Durban is the busiest in South Africa and the third busiest container port in the southern hemisphere.

Near their moorings was the hospital ship the *Sumatra*, and at daybreak Churchill visited her to look for friends. He found several, who all predicted a prolonged struggle. The correspondents (including Atkins and others who had joined them at Cape Town) also learnt that Ladysmith had been cut off. At seven o'clock they travelled inland to Pietermaritzburg in the extra coach of a special mail train.

Although Churchill doesn't mention it, the route took them through the

Durban Harbour at the time of the Boer War

The Valley of a Thousand Hills, seen from the Durban side

A steam train travels through the Valley of a Thousand Hills

spectacular Valley of a Thousand Hills, described by Alan Paton in his novel *Cry, The Beloved Country* as 'grass-covered and rolling, and … lovely beyond any singing of it'. Climbing steadily from the coast, the railway line went past the old Botha's Hill village, Inchanga and Umlaas Road. About halfway between Durban and Pietermaritzburg, Inchanga Station was completed in 1895 and known in those days as the Halfway House. The railway line linking Durban and Pietermaritzburg was completed in 1880, but owing to the mountainous terrain its construction took no less than four years.

Pietermaritzburg is only sixty miles from Durban, but because of the many inclines in the hilly terrain, the journey took four hours in those days. Private Frederick Tucker, who travelled the route on 25 November 1899, described the railway as

a marvel of engineering, sometimes running close to very high precipices and making such quick curves it almost takes one's breath away, especially when running down the steep inclines. The countryside, through which it winds, is very hilly, from the high peaks one could see the marvellous scenery stretched below. Game is very plentiful; deer in abundance. At several places along the line we saw immense quantities of arum lilies growing wild.[3]

By the time Churchill arrived in Pietermaritzburg, military engineers were busy constructing defences around the town. The *Times of Natal* office carried placards with the latest telegrams from the front. In his description of Pietermaritzburg, Churchill wrote:

The town looks more like Ootacamund than any place I have seen. To those who do not know the delightful hill station of Southern India let me explain that Pietermaritzburg stands in a basin of smooth rolling downs, broken frequently by forests of fir and blue gum trees. It is a sleepy, dead-alive place. Even the fact that Colonel Knowle, the military engineer, was busily putting it into a state of defence, digging up its hills, piercing its walls, and encircling it with wire obstructions did not break its apathy.[4]

Botha's Hill Station, completed during the mid-1880s. A hotel on the hill near the station provided meals and overnight accommodation for travellers

Inchanga Station today

British troops at Pietermaritzburg Station

Harriet Road, Pietermaritzburg, *circa* 1900

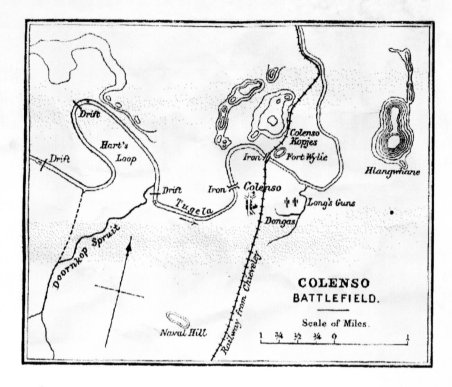

In the meantime, during Churchill's journey, a detachment of Free State Boers had gone on the offensive against British forces at Colenso on 1 November, shelling the Colenso garrison at Fort Wylie from Grobler's Heights until the next evening. Then, during the morning of 3 November, the British garrison retired to Estcourt, which was to be Churchill's next stop. At Pietermaritzburg he found the hospital already full of wounded, among them an old friend from his Cuba and India days, Reggie Barnes, who had been shot through the thigh at close range at Elandslaagte Station. Barnes briefed Churchill about the battle and told him how skilful the Boers were with horse and rifle. That night Churchill travelled on to the village of Estcourt. It had been his intention to get to Ladysmith, where he hoped his old friend Ian Hamilton (the British commander at Elandslaagte) would look after him, but he was too late, as the Boers had already occupied Colenso Station on the Tugela River and held the iron railway bridge. General French and his staff had just slipped through under artillery fire on the last train out of Ladysmith to

The British during action at Colenso

the Cape Colony, where the main cavalry forces were to be assembled. So there was nothing for Churchill to do but wait at Estcourt. Little could he have known that sixty years later he would be granted the freedom of the borough.

Lying among green hills, Estcourt in those days consisted of about 300 detached stone and corrugated-iron houses along two broad streets, extending towards the country. It was a centre for many prosperous farms in the area, where farmers brought their produce to the market and the warehouses. Churchill was surprised at the variety and quantity of goods the shops had to sell.

In Estcourt he found some old friends. Leo Amery was a schoolmate from Harrow from ten years before and one of the war correspondents of *The Times* (and afterwards a colleague of Churchill's in Parliament and government). Together with J.B. Atkins of the *Manchester Guardian*, they took up accommodation in an empty bell tent that stood in the shunting triangle

Estcourt Station, where Churchill pitched his tent

of the railway station, and provided themselves with comforts like a cook, provisions and good wine. Churchill also met Captain Aylmer Haldane, who had helped procure his appointment to Sir William Lockhart's staff during the Tirah Campaign of 1897–98. Wounded at Elandslaagte, Haldane was hoping to rejoin his battalion in Ladysmith. In those early days of the Anglo-Boer War, when Haldane had first arrived at Estcourt, he was attached to the Royal Dublin Fusiliers. 'As the days passed,' Haldane recalled, 'Winston Churchill, who was acting as war correspondent of the *Morning Post*, appeared on the scene, and I spent a good deal of time with him and others of the Press.'[5]

A certain George Clegg was stationmaster at Estcourt, and he allowed Churchill to pitch his tent in his backyard. Clegg recalled how, over drinks in the local bar, the Plough, the young Churchill would regale his audience with his adventures in India and the Sudan. This drew great laughter from Clegg and his friends, who felt Churchill's tales were grossly exaggerated, and they accused him of trying to impress them with tall stories. But Churchill wasn't put off, and in fact told his listeners that he would become British prime minister one day. Clegg's grandson, Derek Clegg, told Churchill's grand-daughter, Celia Sandys, how forty years later George Clegg had read the news of Churchill indeed becoming prime minister and exclaimed, 'By Jove, he's done it!'[6]

At the Plough, Churchill also bought the horse that would be his mount in the area. It seems that Estcourt's horse trader – oblivious to the fact that Churchill had spent quite some time on horseback since his early youth – tried to take him for a ride, so to speak, but soon discovered that the buyer knew more about horses than the seller.

Churchill had in the meantime struck a bargain with a corporal in the Estcourt squadron of the Natal Carbineers, Park Gray,[7] who for a fee of £200 was to guide him through the lines. Gray was a grandson of David Gray, a foreman of a Paisley print works, who had immigrated to South Africa in 1849. According to Gray, the troops had heard that a war corres-pondent was offering £200 to guide him through to Ladysmith, so he decided to look up Churchill. Gray had spent much of his youth game hunting in the Drakensberg and knew most of the country between Estcourt, the Drakensberg and Ladysmith very well. Not only was he keen to earn the money, but was also looking forward to being free from the daily routine of scouting beyond Bergville, Weenen and Mooi River. When he found Churchill in his tent, he formed the impression of 'a lonely … very young Englishman. He had a complexion that many a South African girl would envy and although four years older than I, looked to be 17 or 18.'[8] But Churchill's plan was vetoed by Gray's commanding officer, Major Duncan McKenzie, who had no man to spare for this kind of arrangement.

The days passed slowly and anxiously while cavalry reconnaissance was pushed out every morning for ten or fifteen miles. Sir George White's headquarters

Park Gray in his World War I uniform

were scarcely forty miles away, but between them and Estcourt the Boer commandos were roaming the veld. 'At that time the military began sending an armoured train up to Chieveley and beyond towards Colenso,' commented Park Gray. 'We Colonials could not understand what their object was, nor could we understand why the Boers allowed it.' He was also of the opinion that the British cavalry were ill equipped to deal with the mobile forces the Boers employed.[9]

On 8 November, Churchill had his first experience of travelling in an armoured train, but it had neither conventional guns nor Maxim machine guns; there was no roof to its carriages and no shutters. A company of the Dublin Fusiliers formed the garrison, with half of them in the carriage in front of the engine and the other half behind. Following were three empty wagons with a plate-laying gang and spare rails to mend the line. They travelled from Estcourt towards Colenso, through open grassland with stations every four or five miles, which were merely hamlets consisting of a few corrugated-iron houses amid the endless green hills. The train stopped regularly to question locals and communicate with cyclists and other patrols scouring the countryside. They reached Chieveley, about five miles from Colenso, at around three o'clock; and from there they could see the British Army observation balloon at Ladysmith floating above the distant hills. After a while, the village of Colenso came into view. Situated on the banks of the Tugela River and surrounded by the Drakensberg foothills, it was originally known as Commando Drift before being renamed in honour of the first bishop of Natal, John William Colenso, a missionary who translated the New Testament into Zulu and earned the title 'Sobantu' – Father of the People. A hundred or so dwellings lay below the high hills to the north and a sandbag fort stood on a hill beyond the village. From afar the place looked deserted.

They slowly approached Colenso and came to a stop half a mile before the village. Churchill followed the officer and sergeant, who went on towards the village on foot. Colenso was silent and desolate, the streets littered with the belongings of the inhabitants. Two or three houses had been burnt and the place had evidently been ransacked and plundered by the Boers and local black people. A few of the latter loitered near the far end of the street. The three then made their way back to the railway line, where two lengths of rail

Typical veld around the Tugela River

had been lifted up and thrown over the embankment; broken telegraph wires trailed on the ground. The bridge across the Tugela, however, was undamaged. So they established where the line was broken, that the village was deserted and that the Colenso bridge was safe.

The following day, the party heard the boom of cannons coming from the direction of the besieged town of Ladysmith. Later in the day, they rode out to find some closer listening points as the whole force was making a reconnaissance towards Colenso. Churchill galloped over the hills to the north of the town, and with two companions climbed a high, flat-topped hill. It took them about an hour to reach the summit. From there they had an excellent view – Estcourt was hidden by its surrounding hills, but they

The bridge over the Tugela at Colenso

The Tugela seen from the Colenso bridge

could see Colenso clearly with its corrugated-iron-roofed houses. In the distance to the east lay the spectacular range of the Drakensberg. They saw clouds of smoke from burning grass and other fires in the town, and the military camp of Ladysmith; to the west lay the outline of Bulwana Hill, and they detected a flash from the Boers' Long Tom cannon.

Later, Churchill and his companions were joined by the owner of the nearest farm, a tall, intelligent man with a red beard, before a patrol of the Natal Carbineers also rode up. The patrol had taken great pains to stalk them, hoping they were Boers. The hospitable farmer then invited the group to lunch at his homestead, which, from Churchill's description, was typical of the area:

> The farm stood in a sheltered angle of the hill at no great distance from its summit. It was a good-sized house, with stone walls and a corrugated iron roof. A few sheds and outhouses surrounded it, four or five blue gums afforded a little shade from the sun and a little relief to the grassy smoothness of the landscape. Two women met us at the door, one the wife, the other, I think, the sister of our host. Neither was young, but their smiling faces showed the invigorating effects of this delicious air … Over a most excellent luncheon we discussed many things with these kind people, and spoke of how the nation was this time resolved to make an end of the long quarrel with the Boers, so that there should be no more uncertainty and alarm among loyal subjects of the Queen.[10]

4

Captured by the Boers

'I had not retraced my steps 200 yards when, instead of Haldane and his company, two figures in plain clothes appeared upon the line. Plate-layers, I said to myself, and then with a surge of realization, Boers. My mind retains its impression of these tall figures, full of energy, clad in dark, flapping clothes, with slouch, storm-driven hats, poising on their levelled rifles hardly a hundred yards away. I turned again and ran back towards the engine, the two Boers firing as I ran between the metals.'[1]

O N 14 NOVEMBER, BRITISH PATROLS reported that small parties of Boers were approaching Estcourt from the direction of Weenen and Colenso. The British commander of the lines of communication, Colonel Charles J. Long, made a reconnaissance to ascertain the enemy strength, but it revealed little. It was nevertheless anticipated that a considerable element of the Boer forces around Ladysmith was about to move southwards to attack Estcourt and endeavour to strike Pietermaritzburg. Colonel Long ordered the armoured train at Estcourt to reconnoitre towards Chieveley, with Captain Haldane in command. The order was considered the 'height of folly' by Haldane, who later wrote:

Colonel Charles Long

I may mention that when serving under General Walter Kitchener, the youngest brother of the Field-Marshal of that name, he told me that when, on the 15th November, he heard that the armoured train had been sent on its daily mission, with fuller knowledge than was placed at my disposal as to the strength and disposition of the

Boers, he exclaimed to Colonel Long that in despatching the train that morning he had sent the occupants to their death, and he added that he had no expectation of ever again seeing any of us.[2]

Captain Aylmer Haldane

When Haldane told Churchill on the night of 14 November of the order to send the train, he did not hide his misgivings about the venture, but orders were orders and Haldane was probably keen on possible adventure and engaging the enemy. He invited Churchill to go along. Churchill saw the opportunity for gathering information for his newspaper and, according to his own account, accepted the invitation without hesitation. But Haldane's recollection of his meeting with Churchill, interestingly, contradicts the latter's stated eagerness:

> As I came out of the office feeling rather lugubrious I noticed Churchill, who as well as some other correspondents, was hanging about to pick up such crumbs of information for his newspaper as might be available. I told

British troops boarding an armoured train

him what I had been ordered to do and, aware that he had been out in the train and knew something of the country through which it was wont to travel, suggested that he might care to accompany me next day. Although he was not at all keen he consented to do so, and arranged to be at the station in time for the start.[3]

The train consisted of a company of the Dublin Fusiliers and a company of the Durban Light Infantry in six carriages, sailors from HMS *Terrible* with a small six-pounder naval gun and a break-down gang. It left Estcourt at 5:30 a.m. on 15 November and reached Frere Station about an hour later. 'Frere is merely a station on the line of rail which traverses Natal, and as it consists only of some three or four houses and a few trees it can hardly be dignified by the name of hamlet,' as Sir Frederick Treves, a British surgeon and volunteer during the Anglo-Boer War with the Royal Army Medical Corps, described it in his book. 'Frere is simply a speck – a corrugated iron oasis – on the vast undulating plains of the veldt. These plains roll away to the horizon, and are broken only by kopjes and dongas and the everlasting ant-hills.'[4]

Here a small patrol of the Natal Police reported that they had sighted no enemy within the next few miles. Haldane decided to push on as far as Chieveley, from where an extensive view could be obtained. The grassy country appeared peaceful and deserted, and all was clear as far as Chieveley, but, as

Frere Station

Churchill's South Africa

The rolling hills of northern Natal

the train reached the station, about a hundred Boer horsemen came riding southwards about a mile from the railway line. They were part of General Louis Botha's task force, which had crossed the Tugela River at the Bulwer bridge the day before and had slept near Chieveley.

The telegraphist wired back to Estcourt that parties of Boers were to be seen at no great distance. Colonel Long ordered the train to return to Frere and remain there in observation during the day. But about two miles from Frere, the Boers of the Krugersdorp and Wakkerstroom commandos had occupied a hill that commanded the line, and as the train approached the hill they opened fire with two large field guns, a Maxim and their rifles. The steel sides of the truck in which Churchill found himself rang out with the clatter of bullets and he heard a series of sharp explosions. It was the first time he had seen or heard shrapnel in war. Ahead, the railway line curved round the base of a hill and descended a steep gradient, and the Boer guns had only time for one shot before the train swung round the curve out of their sight.

General Louis Botha's Boers at Chieveley, November 1899

But that was not the end of their troubles. As the engine ran down the steep incline, it hit rocks that had been placed on the rails by the Boers. The engine stayed on the rails, but the first wagon was derailed, killing and injuring some of the plate-layers in it, while the next two armoured wagons with the Durban Light Infantry were also both derailed, and lay jammed against each other, blocking the escape path of the rest. The men of the Durban Light Infantry were shaken and some severely injured, but found shelter from the Boer fire behind the overturned trucks. Churchill and Haldane quickly assessed their situation and agreed that Haldane with the naval gun and his Dublin Fusiliers would try to contain the Boers' fire, while Churchill would go and see what damage had been caused to the train and railway line, and whether there was any chance of clearing the wreckage.

Haldane later recorded:

I knew him well enough to realise that he was not the man to stand quietly by and look on in a critical situation, and it flashed across my mind that he could not be better employed than in a semi-military sense such as he

The armoured train 'Hairy Mary' with its driver, Charles Wagner (right)

suggested … I therefore gladly accepted Churchill's offer and directed
him to undertake what he proposed. His self-selected task, into which
he threw all his energy, was carried out with pluck and perseverance,
and his example inspired the plate-layers, the driver of the locomotive
[one Charles Wagner], and others to work under the fire which the Boers
were directing on the train.[5]

Using the engine as a ram, they managed to push and pull the two wrecked
carriages clear of the railway line, and it was decided that the engine should
go slowly back along the line with all the wounded and that the Dublin and
Durban men should retreat on foot, sheltering themselves behind the engine.
But as the engine's pace increased, the infantry on foot began to lag behind.
Churchill finally forced the engine driver to stop but by then they were already
300 yards ahead of their infantry, close to the bridge across the Blue Krantz
River. He told Wagner to cross the bridge and wait on the other side, and
went back along the railway line to fetch Haldane and the Dublin Fusiliers.
Churchill recalled:

I had not retraced my steps 200 yards when, instead of Haldane and his
company, two figures in plain clothes appeared upon the line. Plate-layers,
I said to myself, and then with a surge of realization, Boers. My mind
retains its impression of these tall figures, full of energy, clad in dark,
flapping clothes, with slouch, storm-driven hats, poising on their levelled
rifles hardly a hundred yards away. I turned again and ran back towards
the engine, the two Boers firing as I ran between the metals.[6]

Churchill found himself in a small cutting with banks about six feet high on
either side where he had no cover, and ran between the lines while, according
to his own accounts, shots were flying past his head, before scrambling up the
bank and through a wire fence. A former public relations officer of Pretoria
City Council, L.P.H. Behrens, however, wrote in an article in *The Star* of
30 April 1960 that there was no evidence that shots had been fired at Churchill.

Hiding in a small depression outside the cutting, he weighed his options.
Fifty yards away was a small plate-layer's masonry cottage with good cover,
and 200 yards away the rocky gorge of the Blue Krantz River. Determined to
make a dash for the river, he got up but the next moment a Boer horseman
came galloping up, ordering him to surrender. In spite of his correspondent's
status, Churchill had taken his Mauser pistol with him, but when he reached
for it, it was not there, as he had taken it off when trying to clear the line,
jumping in and out of the engine. On his horse, the Boer had Churchill in
his rifle targets, and watched the Englishman weighing up whether to make
a run for the river or the plate-layer's hut. But when Churchill realised he
had no chance of escape and that the Boer would not miss at such a distance,
he raised his hands and surrendered.

The Boer aimed a few last shots at the retreating engine and the few
straggling British soldiers, according to Churchill, then remounted and plodded back in the pouring rain with Churchill at his side to where the young
correspondent had left Captain Haldane and his company. The Boers had captured Haldane along with fifty-three non-commissioned officers and troops.
It took them until nightfall to bury the dead. In total, five British soldiers were
killed and forty-five wounded, with a further twenty wounded and seventy
unwounded who escaped with the engine. Of the Durban Light Infantry,

two were killed, one died of his wounds, twenty-five were wounded and nineteen captured, of whom eight were wounded.

Scouting down towards Weenen from Estcourt, a patrol of Natal Carbineers – including Park Gray – had heard the firing of the Boer guns, one of them exclaiming, 'The Boers have got that silly armoured train at last.' They rode back to Estcourt but, on arrival, about a hundred cavalry from both the Carbineers and the Imperial Light Horse were ordered to gallop towards Ennersdale. Gray recalled that they halted at the Little Bushman's railway bridge, where the armoured train had arrived with the wounded men hanging on to every part of the engine, even the cow catcher. From there, the mounted men galloped on to Ennersdale and Heavitree, near Frere, where they had a skirmish with the Boers, but there were few casualties on either side.[7]

There have been several claims made as to who actually captured Winston Churchill that day. In *My Early Life*, Churchill mentions a meeting with the Boer generals that took place three years after his capture. The generals visited England to secure a loan to help their devastated country, and at a private luncheon Churchill was introduced to their leader, General Louis Botha, one of the Boer heroes of the Natal Campaign. They were talking about Churchill's capture when General Botha pointed out that it was he who had taken him prisoner. 'Don't you recognise me?' Botha asked. 'I was that man. It was I who took you prisoner. I, myself.'

In response to this claim, Churchill remarked that Botha, in his white shirt and frock coat, looked very different in all respects from the man he had seen capture him, except for his stature and dark complexion. Later, however, in his writings, Churchill did not doubt that it had indeed been Louis Botha, whom he greatly admired as a soldier and statesman.[8] Botha had taken part in the invasion of Natal as an ordinary burgher but ended the war as a general. To have been captured by the great man himself surely made a dramatic story, and one suspects that while Churchill in his heart knew it had not been Botha, he persisted with this version for literary effect.

The author of *The Man Who Captured Churchill*, Isak Heath, however, provides a different version of exactly how and where Churchill was captured. In May 1984, Heath inherited three volumes of telegrams and other documents from an aunt, Agatha Oosthuizen, the youngest daughter of General

Sarel François Oosthuizen, still only a field cornet with the Krugersdorp commando at the time of the incident. Heath had served as an ambassador and high commissioner to Swaziland, and completed his book in 2000. In it he alleges that Oosthuizen captured Churchill, a detail that is corroborated by a telegram sent by Captain Danie Theron, the master Boer scout who had taken part in this ambush. Theron sent a report to the secretary of state in Pretoria on 28 November 1899, which reads as follows (translated):

General Louis Botha, the man in charge of the Boers who might have captured Churchill and his comrades

> Respectfully I wish to inform about complete reports in the *Natal Witness* and *Natal Mercury* of the 17th of this month regarding the active and prominent role of newspaper correspondent Winston Churchill in the fight with the armoured train at Frere Station. According to *Volksstem* and *Standard and Diggers News* he now pretends that he had no part in the fight, which are all lies. He also refused to stand still when Field Cornet Oosthuizen warned him to surrender, only when he [Oosthuizen] took aim at him did he surrender. As far as I am concerned, Churchill is one of the most dangerous prisoners in our custody. The Natal newspapers have turned him into a big hero.[9]

This telegram was also referred to by Kenneth Griffith in *Thank God We Kept the Flag Flying*: 'A famous young Boer hero named Danie Theron put the hat on it for Winston's hopes of an easy release: T.D. ZAR 28.11.1899 From Captain Theron, i/c Dispatch-riders, Colenso, To Secretary of State, Pretoria ...'[10]

C.J. Barnard, author of *Generaal Louis Botha op die Natalse Front, 1899–1900*, also states that 'this Field-Cornet [Oosthuizen] with his red hair, full beard and ruddy complexion indeed deserves the acknowledgement for Churchill's capture'.[11]

Because of his appearance, Oosthuizen acquired the nickname Rooi (Red) Sarel. Fearless and a true warrior, he was known among his men as Die Rooi Bul (The Red Bull). Born in 1868 on a farm near Pretoria, Sarel took part in the siege of the town during the First Anglo-Boer War (1880–1881) and fought with the Waterval and Doornkop commandos during the Jameson Raid. During the Second Anglo-Boer War, he was a field cornet with the Krugersdorp commando and was wounded three times. Promoted to commandant, he took part in the battles of Colenso and Spioen Kop, and was

General (Rooi) Sarel Oosthuizen, one of several Boers suggested to have captured Churchill

promoted to general after the Battle of Pieter's Hill. He died from wounds received at the Battle of Dwarsvlei on 11 July 1900, after unwisely refusing treatment from the British. Described by General Jan Smuts as 'one of the smartest and bravest men in the whole Boer army ... dashing and impetuous',[12] he surely sounded like the kind of man Churchill should not have attempted to tangle with. And one has to ask how he could have mistaken 'Rooi' Sarel for the dark-featured Louis Botha. If it indeed was Oosthuizen, that is – because a third and a fourth Boer also seem to be in the running for the 'honour' of having captured Churchill.

In Louis Botha's biography by Johannes Meintjies, it is said that Botha was in fact about twenty miles from the scene at the time, and that 'the man who really captured Churchill at Chieveley seems to have been a tall slender Boer called Chris van Veijeren – according to Dr J.H. Breytenbach, who went to great trouble to get to the root of the matter'. Van Veijeren was a member of the Krugersdorp commando, and gave an account of what happened on the day. His statement is held in the State Archives in Pretoria.[13]

But this is not the end of the matter. In his Anglo-Boer War autobiography, *Vir Vryheid en vir Reg* (1941), General Jan Kemp, whose commando ambushed the train, recorded yet another version of what happened (translated from Afrikaans):

> By six o'clock in the morning we were waiting for the armoured train we had already seen the previous morning during a reconnaissance. As the train had passed our position, a few of the men just had time to thrust a few iron poles between the rails when the train started coming back. The locomotive, now in front, jumped across the obstacles, but the next truck derailed, so that the whole train came to a standstill. A well-aimed Krupp shell blew coals of fire from the loco's engine. That didn't deter the drivers, however. They disengaged the loco and fled to Chieveley. We took prisoner the crew of the train.
>
> A few of them tried to run away to Chieveley, but Frans Changuion, Dolf de la Rey and his brother, two brothers Kok, Du Plessis and Van der Nest pursued those fleeing and captured them.
>
> Among them there was a little man ['*'n mannetjie*'] who ran towards the one side when fleeing. When the others surrendered, he also approached at the command of his officer. Frans Changuion said he came walking along like a young ox, or rather a fat schoolboy. This fat bloke told Changuion that the Boers could not take him prisoner, because he was after all the son of Lord Randolph Churchill, and not a Khaki, but a war correspondent for the *Morning Post*.
>
> 'That's all right,' Changuion said to him. 'You're the bugger we want. You are causing all the trouble.'
>
> I want to emphasise that the men who had captured Churchill were those I have mentioned above. Any other persons who claim this doubtful honour for themselves are guilty of twisting historical facts.[14]

A Dutchman from The Hague, Frits Stam, also claimed to have taken Churchill prisoner. In a newspaper interview, Stam said (translated from Dutch): 'I took charge of the correspondent. Although the lad ['*knaap*'] was wearing civilian clothes, I had to search him because you never know. The man was named Winston Churchill and he protested heavily. But when I took two revolvers from his pockets, he quickly gave up. He was transported to Pretoria.'[15] In the same report, mention is also made of a Pretoria burgher, Jaap Botha, who was named as the man who had captured Churchill, but he appears to have just been part of the group of Boers on the scene.

Churchill's capture and the events that followed had a significant bearing on his life, as they launched him into the public eye. By his own admission, it suited him well to have been caught because it gave him the opportunity to escape, made him a British hero in the eyes of certain people, provided him with material for writing books and eventually got him into Parliament in 1900.

Captain Haldane confirmed this shortly after the event, when Churchill conveyed the same message to him: 'At this time we were all feeling, not unnaturally, very disconsolate, but Churchill must have been cheered by the thought, which he communicated to me, that what had taken place, though it had caused the temporary loss of his post as war correspondent, would help considerably in opening the door for him to enter the House of Commons.'[16]

It is also interesting that Haldane indirectly blamed his correspondent friend for the misfortune and loss of lives:

> I do not wish to lay blame on anyone but myself, but had I been alone and not had my impetuous young friend Churchill with me, who in many things was prompted by Danton's motto, *de l'audace, et encore de l'audace et toujours de l'audace* [audacity, more audacity, and ever more audacity], I might have thought twice before throwing myself into the lion's jaws by going almost to the Tugela. But I was carried away by his ardour and departed from an attitude of prudence, which in the circumstances was desirable considering that we were confronting a force which was in the process of invading British territory.[17]

Years later, Churchill still criticised Colonel Long for his decision to send out the armoured train under the circumstances. Describing the ambush incident in his telegraphic report, General Buller also concluded, 'I have called for explanation, as it is impossible to understand such inconceivable stupidity.' And in the subsequent Court of Inquiry, he commented: 'I am of the opinion that the blame for the occurrence rests entirely on Colonel Long.'

On 6 December 1899, a small graveyard was consecrated to those who fell at Chieveley. Over 2 000 troops were present, and the Dublin Fusiliers, who with the Durban Light Infantry had borne the brunt of the encounter, were the last to march past in honour of their comrades. The monument near Chieveley commemorating the wreck of the armoured train and the capture of Churchill was originally erected in 1917. The inscription reads: 'This marks the place where the armoured train was wrecked and the Rt. Hon. Winston Churchill captured by Boer Forces Nov. 15th 1899.'

Ten days after the incident, Private Frederick Tucker wrote in his diary:

One landmark of great interest to us all was the scene of the armoured train disaster which occurred on 15 November. A visit to it and the graves of those who were killed was considered an item not to be missed. The grave itself was a work of art from a soldier's point of view – the lettering was done in a rather novel manner – the letters were formed with empty cartridge cases cemented together, they were the same ones used by the heroes who defended the train. The grave looked very neat, stones had been cut and placed around the sides forming a square.[18]

The name of Winston Churchill is not mentioned anywhere in his entry. But back in Britain, the press was making much of Churchill's role during the Boers' ambush of the armoured train. On 18 November, the *Saturday Herald* published a drawing of Churchill with his hand on the shoulder of a British soldier in front of him. The caption read: 'Young Churchill, a newspaper correspondent, at the battle of the armoured train, was obliged to seize a rifle and give the demoralised English soldiers a brave example. "Can't ye stand like men!" was his scornful cry.'[19]

But others, like Henry du Pré Labouchere, writing in *Truth*, questioned this portrayal:

The train was upset and Mr Churchill is described as having rallied the force by calling out 'Be men! Be men!' But what can officers have been doing who were in command of the attachment? Again, were the men

The memorial commemorating Churchill's capture near Chieveley

showing signs of behaving otherwise than as men? Would officers in command on the battlefield permit a journalist to 'rally' those who were under their order?[20]

On 18 November, Churchill wrote to his mother, telling her in typically dramatic fashion that he had been captured in the armoured train at Frere with officers, soldiers and other non-combatants, while being unarmed and in possession of press accreditation. He also added that she didn't need to be anxious but trusted that she would do all in her power to procure his release.

5

Prisoner of war in Pretoria

*'What men they were, these Boers! I thought of them as I had
seen them in the morning riding forward through the rain –
thousands of independent riflemen, thinking for themselves,
possessed of beautiful weapons, led with skill, living as they
rode without commissariat or transport or ammunition column,
moving like the wind, and supported by iron constitutions and a
stern, hard Old Testament God who should surely smite the
Amalekites hip and thigh. And then, above the rain storm that
beat loudly on the corrugated iron, I heard the sound of a chaunt.
The Boers were singing their evening psalm, and the menacing
notes – more full of indignant war than love and
mercy – struck a chill into my heart…'[1]*

ONCE THE BOERS HAD DISARMED and rounded up the prisoners
captured after the destruction of the armoured train, they counted
fifty-six unwounded or slightly wounded men in addition to the more serious
casualties lying at the scene of the fight. The prisoners sat in the rain, eating
chocolate dug from their pockets, for they had had no breakfast. They were
then ordered to march over the low hills that surrounded the area of their
capture, from where Churchill could see the engine steaming away beyond
Frere Station, so at least something had been saved from the ruin.

Churchill was surprised at their subsequent treatment at the hands of the
Boers, from whom he had expected harshness and humiliation. The British
were told that they did not need to walk fast, while another Boer, seeing
Churchill without a hat in the rain, tossed him an Irish Fusiliers cap, obviously
taken from some British soldier near Ladysmith. After a while, they reached

the Boer guns that had fired on them earlier. Men of the Transvaal State Artillery, dressed in uniform with blue facings, approached them, and the commander, Adjutant Roos, was almost apologetic about their capture. In the meantime, the Boers had searched among the wreckage for the dead and wounded, and a few of the wounded were brought in. The Boers said that they had buried five dead, sent ten seriously wounded to Ladysmith, and kept three severely wounded in their own field ambulances, while a further sixteen severely wounded British soldiers had escaped on the train engine.

After a while, the prisoners had to march on, and looking over the crest of the hill through the driving rain, Churchill saw a large force of Boers marching south led by General Piet Joubert, presumably to attack Estcourt or Mooi River. The prisoners were then taken to a makeshift tent that had been put up in a hollow in one of the hills, which they concluded was General Joubert's headquarters. Churchill explained to the Boers that he was a special correspondent and asked to see General Joubert; his credentials were taken from him by a field cornet, who promised to give them to

A Boer laager at Colenso

Joubert. While they were waiting, a Boer of Scottish descent asked Churchill if he was the son of Lord Randolph Churchill. He confirmed that he was. The revelation prompted a lot of talking among the Boers. Churchill reiterated that he was a newspaper correspondent and that he ought not to be held prisoner, but the Scottish Boer laughed and said, 'Oh, we do not catch lords' sons every day!'[2]

Churchill's desire to be brought before General Joubert came to nothing as the prisoners were ordered to march away towards Colenso under escort of about twenty horsemen. They marched for six hours in the rain across slippery fields, soaked to the skin, before they eventually saw the roofs of Colenso in the distance. They were ordered into a corrugated-iron shed near the station, where they collapsed exhausted. The Boers allowed them to dry themselves by two fires and gave them freshly slaughtered beef to toast on sticks over the flames. Some Boers occupying Colenso came to look at the prisoners, and Churchill had a conversation with two of them, who were brothers, English by race but Boers by choice. One of them took off his blanket, which he was wearing with a hole through the middle like a poncho, and gave it to Churchill to sleep in. He was a thirty-year-old field cornet, Benjamin Raubenheimer, who had taken part in the Battle of Talana. He remembered Churchill as 'a nice young man to talk to who never gave any trouble'.[3]

That night Churchill could not sleep. It was cold and his clothes were wet, and his spirit low. The rain was beating heavily on the roof of the shed. He lay thinking of the rights and wrongs and fortunes of the war, and about the Boers – what they were fighting for, their toughness, skill in the veld and great mobility. For once he despaired of the empire, and it was only at day-break, when the sun came filtering through the shed windows and displaced the chill of the rainy night, that he regained his perspective.

That morning they marched off again, after having had some more meat and rainwater for breakfast. They crossed the wagon bridge over the Tugela River, followed the road and soon reached the hills. They trekked through the hills for several hours, wading across gullies in spate from the heavy rains. Once they halted at a small Boer field hospital tucked away in a deep hollow, consisting of a dozen tents and wagons with large red-cross flags. They

Meal time in the Boer laager

passed through Pieters then on to Nelthorpe, and they began to approach the Boer lines around Ladysmith, where they came to a strong picket and were ordered to halt and rest. Once again, Churchill got into conversation with some of the curious Boers before the prisoners were ordered to march again. They began to move eastwards towards Bulwana Hill, descending into the valley of the Klip River, from where they could spot the British Ladysmith balloon scarcely two miles away. They forded the Klip River and marched on towards the Boer laagers behind Bulwana, which they reached after about ten hours' marching. Here they were given some tea and bully beef, and Churchill and the captured officers (including Haldane and T.H.C. Frankland) were invited to take shelter in the Boer field cornet's tent. Again the inquisitive Boers found an opportunity to have long conversations with Churchill and the others about the reasons for the war.

Towards evening, the commandant asked them to withdraw to some tents that had been pitched at the corner of the laager. There was a special tent for the officers, who for the first time were separated from their men. At this point, Churchill had to decide whether he would pass as an officer or as a private; he settled for officer. As daylight faded, Bulwana Hill threw a dark shadow over the Boer camp. He now witnessed a typical Boer laager scene at the end of a day. The wagons were arranged to form a square, with variously shaped tents and rows of oxen on the inside. Small fires sprang up all around as the Boers started preparing their suppers, and they sat in groups making conversation and smoking their pipes.[4]

Churchill began devising plans to escape, but, observing all the sentries, eventually abandoned the idea. Early the next morning, Commandant Loffie Davel roused the prisoners and they were served tea and bully beef, which Davel presented with an apology for the plainness of the breakfast, and explained that the Boers had nothing better to eat themselves. After breakfast they marched off to Elandslaagte Station, over the hills towards the north, and skirted the Boer picket line around Ladysmith to the left. Every half a mile or so, the road led through or passed close to Boer laagers, and they reached Elandslaagte Station at around eleven o'clock. Here a train awaited the prisoners, with about six closed wagons for the privates and a first-class carriage for the officers. Churchill was seated in the carriage; there were two armed Boers guarding them, and the doors were locked. Before their departure, a festering wound on Churchill's hand, which appears to have been sustained during the attack on the train, was attended to by a young doctor named Thomas Visser, who also headed up the ambulances.[5] This time the prisoners received a decent meal of preserved mutton and fish, loaves of bread, jam and tea. At about noon, the train steamed off and later Captain Haldane pointed out to Churchill the ridge of Elandslaagte where the British had defeated the Boers under General Kock on 21 October.

One of the two Boer guards was called Spaarwater, a farmer from the Ermelo district, with whom Churchill had a long conversation about the war. He had fired more than 100 rounds at the armoured train, for which he earned a fortnight's leave to visit his wife, as opposed to some costly war decoration. Churchill wrote a note, which he dated and signed: 'The Bearer, H.G. Spaarwater, has been very kind to me and British officers captured in the Estcourt armoured train. I shall be personally grateful to anyone who may be

Elandslaagte Station, from where the prisoners were sent to Pretoria

able to do him any service should he himself be taken prisoner.' (Spaarwater was killed in action the following year, but a century later the note was still in the possession of his granddaughter, Martha Bam.)

The other guard, who sat opposite Churchill for the whole train journey, was nineteen-year-old Daniël Swanepoel, from Krugersdorp. He brought Churchill a cup of coffee at Elandsfontein Station (now Germiston), which Swanepoel thought was made from potatoes, but which Churchill seemed to enjoy nevertheless. In later years, Swanepoel became a prominent Johannesburg businessman and corresponded regularly with Churchill.

Another guard on the train – a bearded man who spoke little English – appears to have been the Boer who placed the rocks on the rails that derailed the armoured train. They were later joined by the ticket collector, an eloquent Dutchman, one of many in the employ of the railways at the time. The

Daniël Swanepoel (right), who guarded Churchill on the train to Pretoria

afternoon went by before the train passed near Dundee and Talana Hill, and later the Majuba Mountain, famous as the site of the main battle of the First Anglo-Boer War, which they saw just as night was closing in. It was dark when the train reached Volksrust; here Boers and locals stared at the British prisoners. Churchill had a conversation with a sixteen-year-old Boer by the name of Cameron, whose father had come to South Africa from Scotland. To Churchill's question as to why he was fighting the British, Cameron replied that it couldn't be helped – his home was South Africa.

They left Volksrust and it was midday on 18 November, a fine sunny day, when the prisoners eventually reached the Transvaal capital, Pretoria. Approximately thirty miles north of Johannesburg, the town lies at an altitude of about 1350 metres above sea level in a warm valley surrounded by the hills of the Magaliesberg range. Pretoria is known for its humid subtropical climate, and residents suffer in the heat of summer, as Churchill and his fellow men were to discover during their imprisonment there.

The train with the prisoners pulled into a siding with an earth platform that gave onto the streets of the town. There was a large crowd awaiting them, consisting of burghers and women with parasols, and others just loafing about; South African Republic Police officers in white helmets were waiting in a line. The soldiers were ordered off the train, to the clicking of cameras, and told to form up in rank. There was a twenty-minute wait, during which Churchill contemplated his hatred of the real enemy, who were not the Boers fighting at the front, but the petty and contemptible officials of all nationalities.

Churchill was led away by a tall, unshaven police sergeant, who told him that he was not an officer and that he had to join the common soldiers, and was led across the open space where the men were formed in a column. Fortunately, Field Cornet Malan, apparently a close relative of President Paul Kruger, then came up and led him back to the group of officers. The prisoners were finally marched off – the soldiers to an enclosed camp on the racecourse, and the four officers to the Staatsmodelskool, on Skinner and Van der Walt streets.[6] The school had been converted into a prison during the war. They were marched along two sandy avenues of detached houses before reaching the school, a long, red-brick building with a slate verandah

Churchill (extreme right) with a group of prisoners

and a row of iron railings. On the verandah, bearded men in khaki uniform were smoking, reading and talking. The contingent passed through the iron gates of the prison, where they learnt there were sixty other British officers in Boer custody, taken prisoner during the early clashes of the war, mainly at Nicholson's Nek. These officers immediately tried to catch up on General Buller's advance and the latest news from the front.

Churchill's room was at the front of the building, facing Van der Walt Street, but he often slept on the verandah when the summer nights were too hot. The Transvaal government provided a daily ration of bully beef and groceries, and the prisoners were allowed to purchase their other essentials from a local storekeeper, a Mr Boshof. On their arrival, each officer was given a new set of clothes, bedding, towels and toilet necessaries.

By the time Churchill got to Pretoria, his mother, who was staying at

Churchill's South Africa

The Staatsmodelskool in Pretoria where Churchill was held captive

Esrick Park in Yorkshire, had received a telegram two days before signed by Moreton Frewin, which read: 'Unpleasant news capture hundred men from armoured train Ladysmith.' The same evening, she received further news from the *Morning Post*: 'I regret to inform you that Mr Winston Churchill has been captured by the Boers. He fought gallantly after an armoured train in which he was travelling had been trapped.' Churchill's servant, Thomas Walden, also wrote a letter to Lady Randolph to inform her that her son had been taken prisoner. Walden added that Colonel Long believed that there was 'no braver gentleman in the Army'.[7]

Transvaal war secretary, Louis de Souza, whom Churchill found friendly and obliging

On reaching Pretoria, Churchill immediately demanded his release from the Transvaal government on the grounds that he was a press correspondent and not a combatant. But the Natal newspapers had published glowing accounts of his role in the incident involving the train and the wounded, and General Joubert therefore argued that even if he had not fired a shot himself, he had harmed the Boer operations and should be treated as a prisoner of war.

Custody of the British officers was the responsibility of a board of managers, four of whom visited the officers regularly. Churchill regarded Louis de Souza, the war secretary, as the most friendly and obliging. Then there was a Dr Gunning, an amiable, fat little Dutchman, who also managed the State Museum; Commandant R.W.L. Opperman; and Field Cornet Malan, the man who had spared Churchill from being sent to the racecourse with the privates. Despite this, Churchill and Malan harboured an intense dislike for each other. Malan was later captured by the Khakis in August 1901 and sent to Ceylon as a prisoner of war.

Thus started the most monotonous and miserable period of Churchill's life. It was summer on the Highveld, the rooms were stuffy and early in the sultry mornings the soldier-servants, who were prisoners themselves, would bring coffee; sitting up in bed, the men would smoke cigarettes and cigars. Breakfast, which according to Churchill was not a pleasant meal, was served at nine. They would pass the long mornings reading and playing chess or cards. At one o'clock, lunch was served, which was the same as breakfast. Then came the long, boring afternoon. Some of the officers used to play rounders in the small yard for exercise, while the rest walked up and down, looking over the railings at the passers-by in the street.

Churchill found it difficult to write, as the ink seemed to dry quickly, and he could not read for long periods. During the month of his captivity, he only read Carlyle's *History of Friedrich II of Prussia, Called Frederick the Great* and Mill's *On Liberty*. At the end of the day, he used to walk up and down the courtyard watching the guards, trying to figure out some way of escaping. With darkness approaching, electric lamps were switched on and the courtyard was lit up, before the bell called them for their last meal of the day in the dining hall. Around the table, the stories of the officers' capture at Talana and Nicholson's Nek were repeated endlessly.

In the room next to Churchill's, James Gage Hyde was held, a civilian prisoner whose father, George Clarence Hyde, had treated the wounded after the Battle of Rorke's Drift during the Zulu War of 1879. James Hyde owned a farm at the foot of Tchrengula Hill and at the Battle of Nicholson's Nek on 30 October 1899 had joined in with the Irish Fusiliers. Captured by the Boers during the rout, he was sent to the Staatsmodelskool as a prisoner of war. During Churchill's captivity, he and Hyde used to recite poetry – Longfellow, Shakespeare and Macaulay. This confused the guards who could not understand what they were saying. Hyde warned Churchill about the dangers of trying to escape, but Churchill always dismissed them.

About ten days after his arrival in Pretoria, Churchill received a visit from the American consul, Mr Macrum, from whom he learnt that there was some uncertainty back home as to whether he was alive, wounded or unharmed. An old American friend of Churchill, Senator Bourke Cockran, had telegraphed from New York to the United States' representative in Pretoria to determine how Churchill's case stood. Before long, however, Churchill realised that Macrum's sympathies lay with the Transvaal government.

During this time, the officers also learnt that the Boers had been beaten at Belmont Station and at Graspan, and that there was fighting at Modder River. These actions were part of Lord Methuen's drive along the western railway line to relieve Kimberley, then still besieged by the Boers.

Deneys Reitz, who would later become well known as author of *Commando: A Boer Journal of the Boer War*, recalled that he visited the Staatsmodelskool with his father, the Transvaal secretary of state, and that one of the prisoners – who turned out to be Churchill – had asked for an interview:

> We passed through the sentries into a large classroom where he was playing games with his fellow-prisoners. His name was Winston Churchill, a son of Lord Randolph Churchill, of whom I had often heard. He said he was not a combatant but a war-correspondent, and asked to be released on that account. My father, however, replied that he was carrying a Mauser pistol when taken, and so must remain where he was. Winston Churchill said that all war-correspondents in the Sudan had carried weapons for self-protection, and the comparison annoyed my father, who told him that the Boers were not in the habit of killing non-combatants. In the end the young man asked my father to take with him some articles which he had written for a newspaper in England and if there was nothing wrong with them to send them on via Delagoa Bay. My father read portions of the articles to us at home that evening, and said that Churchill was a clever young man, in which he was not far wrong, for soon after the prisoner climbed over a wall and escaped out of the Transvaal – how, I never heard.[8]

While imprisoned, Churchill wrote two letters, one to the war secretary and one to General Joubert. According to Churchill, he never received an answer to either of these applications for release. What he did not mention in his reminiscences was that he had offered, if released by the Transvaal government, to take no further part in the campaign or pass on any information that might harm their cause. In a letter to De Souza, dated 26 November 1899 (four days before his twenty-fifth birthday), he wrote: 'I am willing – though I desire to continue my journalistic work – to give any parole the Transvaal Government may require viz. either to continue to observe non-combatant character or to withdraw altogether from South Africa during the war.'[9] He followed this up with another letter to De Souza on 8 December, promising that, if released, he would 'give any parole that may be required not to serve against the Republican forces or to give any information affecting the military situation'.[10]

At the same time, he attempted to get himself reclassified as a military prisoner, because he had heard of a possible exchange of military prisoners, and requested Lord Milner to have him exchanged for a Boer prisoner. It later transpired that the government had seriously considered accepting his offer, which gave rise to accusations that he had broken his agreement when he continued reporting after his escape to Lourenço Marques. To the Boers, Churchill was an important prisoner because of his role during the armoured train ambush, his reputation as a war correspondent and his status as a member of the British aristocracy.

The well-known Deneys Reitz of *Commando* fame, who accompanied his father, State Secretary F.W. Reitz, to the prison where Churchill was being held

On the day of Churchill's escape, 12 December 1899, General Joubert wrote to the Transvaal secretary of state, F.W. Reitz, that he had no objection to Churchill being set free, but with the postscript, 'Will he tell the truth? Or will he also be a chip off the old block?'[11] – a reference to Sir Randolph and his disparaging views of the Boers.

In the meantime, along with some other officers, Churchill was firmly resolved to escape. They would have to plan it carefully.

6

Escape for Delagoa Bay

'Nearly three hundred miles stretched between me and Delagoa Bay. My escape must be known at dawn. Pursuit would be immediate. Yet all exits were barred. The town was picketed, the country was patrolled, the trains were searched, the line was guarded. I wore a civilian brown flannel suit. I had seventy-five pounds in my pocket and four slabs of chocolate...'[1]

THE STAATSMODELSKOOL LOOKS MUCH THE same today as it did in 1899, but the adjacent dusty roads have now become busy dual carriageways. The school occupied an area of about seventy yards square. On the front and sides, it was enclosed by a chest-high ornamental cast-iron fence, and at the back by six-foot iron railings. These boundaries would normally have offered little obstacle to a young man. However, they were guarded on the inside by armed sentries. To the rear was a grass playground with some tents, the cookhouse and latrines, all separated from the main building by a ten-foot-high wire fence.

Captain Haldane and Sergeant Major A. Brockie had worked out a plan of escape, having discovered that when the sentries near the offices walked about on their beats, they were at certain moments unable to see the top portion of the wall at the back of the school, and that there was a possible escape route through a latrine window to a dark stretch of ground, then over another wall and into the garden of the adjoining property. This property belonged to a Boer general, Lucas Meyer. From here they could make their way to the railway line and jump on a train leaving Pretoria, hoping to reach Lourenço Marques, from where the officers could return to their units. They had already established from railway timetables in the newspapers that a train left the station daily at 11.10 p.m.

Brockie was a former miner from Johannesburg who had joined the Imperial Light Horse and was captured by the Boers on the Klip River. He was a handy man to have around in the event of an escape, as he could speak Dutch and Fanagalo, a pidgin that had developed in the mines from several African languages.

Before Haldane and Brockie could implement their plan, two soldier-servants, David Bridge and Joe Cahill, escaped on 7 December by scaling the fence at exactly the spot that Haldane and Brockie had identified for their escape. Some of the guards knew of the escape, but did not notify the authorities. Cahill was never heard of again, but Bridge was recaptured and imprisoned at Waterval Prison, near Pretoria. He would be freed on 6 June 1900 along with a few thousand other prisoners after the British occupied Pretoria.

Haldane and Brockie therefore had to wait their turn. Because they expected Churchill's early release, they did not include him in their plan. But he insisted on going along. Unfortunately for the three of them, their attempt to escape on the night of 11 December proved futile, as the guard barely moved an inch. So they waited to try again the next night.

They passed another day in suspense. As evening came on Tuesday 12 December, the dinner bell rang and Churchill strolled across the quadrangle before hiding in one of the offices. He watched the guards through a chink, but for half an hour they remained at their posts. Then one guard turned, walked up to the other and they began to talk with their backs to Churchill. This was the moment he had been waiting for. He darted for the wall, grabbed the top and drew himself up. A last glimpse from the top of the wall revealed the guards still talking with their backs turned, a mere fifteen yards away. Churchill lowered himself down into the adjoining garden where he hid among the shrubs.

He now had to wait for Haldane and Brockie. The house was some twenty yards away from where he was hiding, and soon Churchill realised that it was full of people, with brightly lit rooms and figures moving about inside. Churchill's account mentions a man coming out of the door and walking through the garden in his direction, stopping hardly ten yards away from his hiding place. After a while, another man came out of the house, lit a cigar, and both men then walked back. No sooner had they turned than a cat pursued by

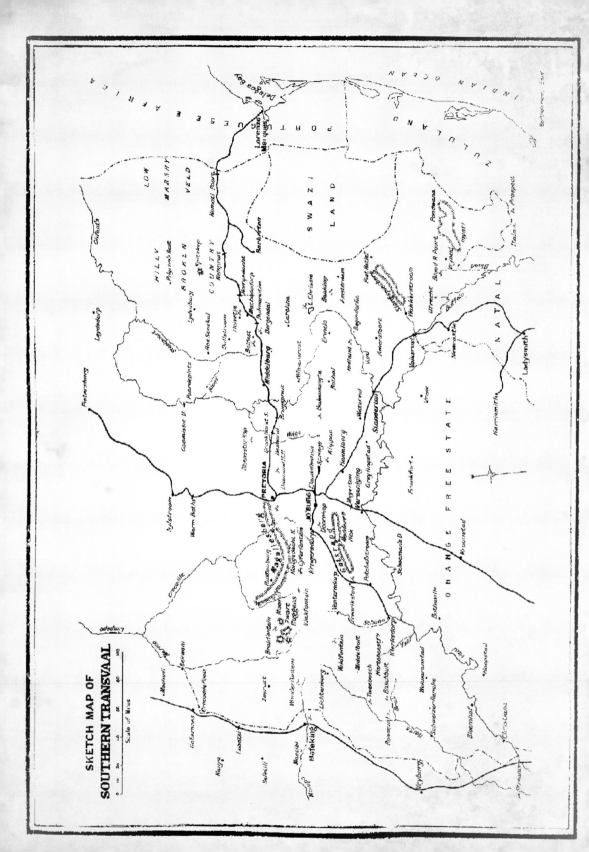

a dog ran into Churchill, and let out a startled meow of fright before darting back again. Both men stopped in their tracks, but then left through the garden gate and went towards the town.[2]

According to Churchill, an hour had passed since he had scaled the prison wall, but still there was no sign of Haldane or Brockie. Then he heard a voice from the quadrangle saying 'all up', and he crawled back to the wall. On the other side, two officers were walking up and down speaking Latin and talking all kinds of nonsense, but Churchill picked up his name. One of the officers then said clearly, 'Cannot get out. The sentry suspects. It's all up. Can you get back again?' Whereupon Churchill replied, 'I shall go on alone.' He strode into the middle of the garden and went through the gate to his left. He passed the sentry – who could not have been very alert – less than five yards away without looking left or right, and soon he was at large in Pretoria.[3]

Brockie survived the Anglo-Boer War along with Churchill and Haldane, but was killed in a mining accident very soon afterwards.

It has to be noted that until Haldane's death in 1950, there was a simmering disagreement between him and Churchill as to the exact events of the night of 12 December. According to Haldane, the three had again agreed to postpone their escape, but Churchill then scaled the wall by himself. In contrast, Churchill's account has him waiting behind the wall for more than an hour for the others before the discussion related above. Haldane agreed that a conversation had taken place, but that Churchill had said that 'he would go without us'. Haldane also added, 'I must admit that I was surprised and disgusted to find myself left in the lurch, for Churchill had walked off with my carefully thought-out plan, though he did not know all the details, and in fact had taken the bread out of my mouth.' When he and Brockie heard that Churchill was already on the other side of the wall, they wanted to follow immediately, but the guard was at his post and they had to wait until he moved off again. Unfortunately for Haldane, the guard saw his upper body rise above the wall against the full moon and ordered him to get down.[4]

Whatever the real circumstances, Churchill was now free and walked down Skinner Street, in the middle of the road, at night-time, pretending to be relaxed. The locals paid him no attention anyway. In his pockets he had four pieces of chocolate and £75. He finally reached the suburbs, crossed a little bridge over the Apies River, which separated Sunnyside from central Pretoria (according to historians there is no written evidence that he claimed that he 'swam the mighty Apies River'), and walked in the direction of the railway. His plan was to find the Delagoa Bay Railway[5] to Lourenço Marques in Portuguese East Africa, which was neutral during the Anglo-Boer War. Not possessing a map or compass, he would follow the line. He came to the railway after having walked south for half a mile, and followed it eastwards at a brisk pace. Along the way he had to make short detours to avoid the line pickets, whose fires gleamed in the night, as well as the bridge guards. At the time, railway lines in the area were mostly guarded by the garrison division of the volunteer Hollander Corps.

After walking for about two hours, Churchill saw the lights of the first station, and leaving the line, circled around it. Assuming that the next train would halt there, he hid in a ditch some 200 yards further on, from where he would jump on board before it picked up speed. According to Haldane, this was a station called Muckleneuk. Just an hour later, a goods train arrived, waited for five minutes and then steamed off again. As the train departed, Churchill made a dash for the carriages, but by this time the train had worked up quite a bit of steam. He hurled himself onto a carriage, grabbed a hand-hold and managed to seat himself on the couplings of the fifth carriage from the front of the train. The wagons were full of sacks covered in coal dust, and he burrowed in among them. Lying there in hiding, he wondered where the train was heading and whether it was indeed the Delagoa Bay line he found himself on. But before long, he had fallen asleep among the sacks.

He woke up well before dawn, not knowing how far the train had travelled or where it was. Realising he had to leave the train before daybreak, he positioned himself on the couplings and jumped. He struck the ground in two big strides, then sprawled into the ditch along the line. He was shaken but unhurt. In the dark, he looked around:

> I was in the middle of a wide valley, surrounded by low hills, and carpeted with high grass drenched in dew. I searched for water in the nearest gully, and soon found a clear pool. I was very thirsty, but long after I had quenched my thirst I continued to drink, that I might have sufficient for the whole day.

The Apies River at Daspoort, Pretoria

Presently the dawn began to break, and the sky to the east grew yellow and red, slashed across with heavy black clouds. I saw with relief that the railway ran steadily towards the sunrise. I had taken the right line, after all.

Having drunk my fill, I set out for the hills, among which I hoped to find some hiding-place, and as it became broad daylight I entered a small grove of trees which grew on the side of a deep ravine. Here I resolved to wait till dusk. I had one consolation: no one in the world knew where I was. I did not know myself. It was now four o'clock. Fourteen hours lay between me and the night. My impatience to proceed while I was still strong doubled their length. At first it was terribly cold, but by degrees the sun gained power, and by ten o'clock the heat was oppressive. My sole companion was a gigantic vulture, who manifested an extravagant interest in my condition, and made hideous and ominous gurglings from time to time. From my lofty position I commanded a view of the whole valley. A little tin-roofed town lay three miles to the westward. Scattered farmsteads, each with a clump of trees, relieved the monotony of the undulating ground. At the foot of the hill stood a Kaffir kraal, and the figures of its inhabitants dotted the patches of cultivation or surrounded the droves of goats and cows which fed on the pasture.[6]

Churchill noticed that the railway ran through the middle of the valley, and counted four trains passing each way. He also noted a steep gradient along which the train climbed slowly, and where he thought he could attempt to jump aboard again at night-time. It was hot, and the chocolate that he ate made him very thirsty, but he dared not leave the wood to find water. At times he could see white men riding or walking across the valley, and once a farmer fired two shots at birds near his hiding place. Late in the day, a Boer wagon drawn by a long team of oxen slowly crawled along the dirt road towards the town.

When darkness set in, he hurried back to the railway line, where he waited for some time at the top of the steep gradient for a train to pass by. But he waited in vain, and finally decided to walk on. He walked for about six or seven hours, avoiding the guarded bridges, the labourers' huts and the stations. This was extremely arduous – he collapsed into bogs when he ventured away from the railway line and became tired out from hunger and lack of sleep. Every now and then, he could see the lights of houses, and longed for the comfort and warmth they offered.

He eventually came to a station (Brugspruit) with two or three buildings around it, and three goods trains in the sidings. He contemplated boarding one of the trains immediately and hiding among the freight, but he had no idea of its destination. He crept up to the platform and was busy examining the markings on the trucks when he heard people approaching, so he had no choice but to slip away quietly. He plodded on and after a while saw the glow of fires in the distance. Thinking that the fires were from a kraal, he walked towards them, but after considering the futility of the idea decided against it and retraced his steps down the track. But he soon changed his mind again and set off towards the light of the fires. He was to discover that they were much further away than he had estimated. But finally, between two and three o'clock in the morning, as he got close, he discovered that they were not kraal fires, but the engine furnaces of a coal mine. He could see the outline of a group of houses around the mouth and the wheel of the mine lift. Before his escape he had learnt that in the Witbank and Middelburg mining districts there were English residents, and the thought crossed his mind that he might have stumbled upon friendly territory. It was actually the Brugspruit

The Transvaal & Delagoa Bay Collieries at Witbank where Churchill hid from the Boers

mine, which had opened in 1897 along with a station, Witbank, which became established as a town in 1903.

Churchill writes that he walked up to a single-storey house separated from the other dwellings, and knocked on the door. A light inside came on and someone shouted from a window, '*Wer ist da?*' (It is unlikely that the person spoke German; he was probably asking the question in Dutch, '*Wie is daar?*' and Churchill mistook it for German.) Churchill replied that he had had an accident and needed help. The man who opened the door for him happened to be a certain John Howard, the manager of the Transvaal & Delagoa Bay Collieries, who had become a naturalised burgher of the Transvaal some years before the war. At first, Churchill spun him the story that he was a Dr Bentinck, that he was going to join his commando at Komatipoort, and that he had fallen off a train and dislocated his shoulder.

John Howard,
the mine manager

'I think I'd like to know a little more about this railway accident of yours,' Howard said, whereupon Churchill revealed his real identity and his plans to get to Lourenço Marques. 'Thank God you have come here!' Howard replied. 'It is the only house for twenty miles where you would not have been handed over. But we are all British here, and we will see you through.'[7]

Howard had not been called up to fight against the British and was instead allowed to remain on the mine, to keep it pumped out until mining could be resumed. His father, Fioard Howard, had been a captain in the Royal Engineers. Howard served the hungry Churchill a whisky and soda, a piece of cold leg of mutton and some other food. He then discussed the matter with his colleagues, the mine secretary, John Adams, the mine engineer, Daniel Dewsnap, the mine captain, Joe McKenna, a miner, Joe McHenry, and the mine doctor, James Gillespie. Together they decided that they would help him escape. According to Churchill, he was hidden in a shaft below the winding wheel for the time being. Then he was taken down in a shaft cage, shooting down into the bowels of the earth, as he described it – although, according to one source, the mine was only twenty metres deep.[8] At the bottom, two Scottish miners were waiting with lanterns and a mattress and blankets, and he was finally led to a sort of chamber. Howard gave him candles, a bottle of whisky and a box of cigars. In the meantime, Howard had scared off the black miners from that part of the mine by telling them that a tokoloshe, a mythical, hairy, evil, dwarf-like goblin from African folklore, had been seen there. This, of course, put the fear of the devil into them, and they steered clear.

It appears, however, that Churchill was not hidden in a mine shaft, but rather in the new, as yet unused, underground stables where, in Churchill's own words, 'the air was cool and fresh'.[9] The stables were to be used for the horses that hauled coal trucks up the steep inclines to the hoisting cage.

Churchill wrote that he had the constant company of rats, and could hear the pattering of their feet, but that he was not afraid of them. In a report in *The Star* in 1923, however, Howard said that Churchill had insisted that he would rather the Boers recapture him than spend another night in his hiding place with the rats around him. Howard was therefore obliged to find him alternative accommodation. Ignoring these de-tails, the *Witbank News* wrote that during this time Churchill is said to have amused himself by entic-ing the rats to come closer by offering them scraps of food.[10] According to this newspaper, Churchill is supposed to have spent close to two weeks in the mine, but by Howard's account he spent two days and one night in the newly laid-out stable before he was accommodated in a storeroom in the mine manager's house. And Churchill himself refers to the three days he spent in the mine.

Daniel Dewsnap,
the mine engineer

Unfortunately, today nothing is left of the mining gear, the buildings – including Howard's house – or the railway sidings, all of which were demolished.

On 16 December, Howard told Churchill that he had made plans to get him out of the Transvaal. In the neighbourhood of the mine lived a concession storekeeper, Charles Burnham (but named as 'Burgener' by Churchill), who would be sending a consignment of wool to Delagoa Bay on the 19th. The bales would be loaded into rail wagons at the mine's siding; the siding was conveniently connected with the Delagoa Bay Railway by a branch line. Churchill could then be concealed in a space in the centre of a wagon among the bales. A tarpaulin would be fastened over each wagon and it was unlikely that the fastenings would be removed at the frontier. Churchill himself would have much preferred to go through the veld with a horse and guide, but in the end he accepted Howard and Burnham's proposal.

7

Return to freedom

'All day long we travelled eastward through the Transvaal, and when darkness fell we were laid up for the night at a station which, according to my reckoning, was Waterval Boven ... During all the dragging hours of the day I had lain on the floor of the truck occupying my mind as best I could, painting bright pictures of the pleasures of freedom, of the excitement of rejoining the army, of the triumph of a successful escape but haunted also perpetually by anxieties about the search at the frontier, an ordeal inevitable and constantly approaching.'[1]

WHEN IT WAS DISCOVERED THAT Churchill had escaped, about twelve hours after he scaled the prison wall, the alarm was raised, telegrams with his description were sent to the railways, and trains were searched. In recent years, a telegram sent by the Boer police providing a description of Churchill as an escaped prisoner of war was sold by the famous auctioneer Christie's, which described it as one of the most significant sales of Churchill memorabilia of its kind. It was part of a collection of Churchill material assembled over thirty years by Malcolm S. Forbes Jr, grandson of Bertie Charles Forbes (1880–1954), the Scottish financial journalist and author who founded *Forbes Magazine*. The telegram, sent in December 1899 after Churchill's escape from his prison in Pretoria, reads: 'Englishman 25 years old about 5 foot 8 inches tall medium build walks with a slight stoop. Pale features. Reddish-brown hair almost invisible small moustache. Speaks through his nose and cannot pronounce the letter S. Had last a brown suit on and cannot speak one word of Dutch.'

There is a much-cited story that the Transvaal authorities circulated a 'wanted dead or alive' pamphlet, but this is a misrepresentation. This handbill,

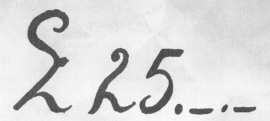

£25.——

(vijf en twintig pond stg.)
belooning uitgeloofd door
de Sub. Commissie van wijk V
voor den Specialen Constabel
dezer wijk, die den ontvluchte
Krijgsgevangene
            Churchill.
levend of dood: te dezer kantore
aflevert.——

        Namens de Sub. Comms.
                        wijk V
        [signature]
                  Sec.

Translation

£25

(Twenty-five Pounds stg) REWARD is offered by the Sub-Commission of the fifth division, on behalf of the Special Constable of the said division, to anyone who brings the escaped prisoner of war

CHURCHILL,

dead or alive to this office.

For the Sub-Commission of the fifth division,
            (Signed) LODK de HAAS, Sec.

NOTE. The Original Reward for the arrest of Winston Churchill on his escape from Pretoria, posted on the Government House at Pretoria, brought to England by the Hon. Henry Massham, and is now the property of W. R. Baylen.

1899

The poster promising a reward for Churchill's capture, dead or alive along with an English translation, was published in *My Early Life* in 1930, and has been reproduced since in a number of biographies of Churchill without questioning its true origin. It is significant that nowhere in this notice do the words 'Zuid-Afrikaansche Republiek' or the name of any government office appear. In reality, the pamphlet was drawn up by a Dutch immigrant, Lodewijk de Haas, a member of the original Hollander Corps in Pretoria.[2] When he was informed of Churchill's escape and instructed that he and his two assistants help find and arrest him, he wrote the note as a kind of joke on a sheet of paper and stuck it on the door of his office. When the British occupied Pretoria on 6 June 1900, it was discovered by an officer and subsequently found its way to London. In 1904 it was offered to Churchill as a souvenir by Roby Burton of North Finchley, and Churchill paid £5 for it. It was portrayed as an authentic document issued by the Transvaal authorities, however, and a translation added to it gave the impression that the handwritten note and typed text constituted an original dead-or-alive warrant. After the outbreak of World War II, De Haas, then living in England, wrote to Churchill and introduced himself as the author of the note four decades after the event. This led to lively correspondence between Churchill and De Haas, which included fourteen letters written by the latter.

After Churchill's escape, all kinds of rumours flew around – one that he had escaped disguised as a woman, another that he had been captured at Komatipoort disguised as a Transvaal policeman, another that he had been captured at Waterval Boven, and others to the effect that he had been arrested at Brugspruit, at Middelburg and at Bronkhorstspruit. It was also alleged that he had changed clothes with a waiter and was hiding in the house of a pro-British citizen in Pretoria. The day after Churchill's escape, his official release, signed by General Joubert, arrived at the Staatsmodelskool. Churchill himself found it hard to believe that the Transvaal government had seriously contemplated his release prior to his escape, arguing that the Boers hated being beaten, even in the smallest things.

At the mine, Churchill was getting ready to be stowed away on a goods train bound for Lourenço Marques. The day before the planned departure passed slowly; Churchill spent the greater part of it reading Scottish author

Robert Louis Stevenson's *Kidnapped*. He could by then well relate to the thrilling escape of the characters David Balfour and Alan Breck in the glens.

While he was reading, he heard rifle shots nearby, and his first thought was that the Boers had arrived. But soon he could hear the sound of voices and laughter coming from Howard's office, whereupon Howard came to tell him that the field cornet of the area, Theuns Pretorius, had visited and said that they had caught Churchill at Waterval Boven the day before. The shots had come from a bottle-shooting contest between the two, and the field cornet won two pounds from Howard, thus leaving in good spirits.

At two o'clock on the morning of 19 December, Churchill was ready and waiting for Howard's signal to leave for the train. When Howard arrived, he beckoned to Churchill and off they went in silence to the siding, where three bogie carriages stood. A gang of black men were busy loading a large bale into the rear wagon; Howard walked to the first wagon. As he crossed the line at the end of the wagon, he gave a signal to Churchill to get on board. Churchill squeezed through a hole between the bales of wool at the end of the wagon and went through a narrow tunnel between the bales to the centre. There he found a space wide enough to lie in, and made himself as comfortable as possible under the circumstances. It was summer on the Highveld, and Churchill would no doubt have felt the heat. Charles Burnham, who had to keep an eye on proceedings, was travelling in the guard's van.

Some three or four hours later, Churchill heard the noise of an approaching engine, followed by bumping and banging as the engine coupled, and finally he was away on a journey that was expected to take sixteen hours. He took stock of his supplies – a revolver (although it was unclear in what way he was going to use it), two roast chickens, some meat, a loaf of bread, a melon and three bottles of cold tea.

He found a narrow chink at the end of the wagon through which he could look at the outside world. He had learnt by heart the names of all the stations en route to the border, which included Witbank, Middelburg, Bergendal, Belfast, Dalmanutha, Machadodorp, Waterval Boven, Waterval Onder, Elands, Nooitgedacht and Komatipoort. At Witbank, the branch line from the mine joined the main railway, and after two or three hours' delay and shunting they coupled to a regular train, and from there proceeded at a faster pace.

The many stations on the railway line between Pretoria and Lourenço Marques

They travelled eastwards through the Transvaal all day and by the evening had reached Waterval Boven, where they laid up for the night. They had completed almost half the journey. Waterval Boven is a small town on the edge of the escarpment on the banks of the Elands River, above the Elands Falls (hence the name, meaning 'above the waterfall' in Dutch). Its sister town of Waterval Onder lies at the base of the escarpment, below the waterfall. Both settlements were established because of the Pretoria–Delagoa Bay railway line, built by the Netherlands-South African Railway Company.[3]

At Waterval Boven, Churchill wanted to sleep, but was worried about snoring while the train was standing in a silent siding, and that he might be discovered by someone. But he fell into a merciful slumber. Between Waterval Boven and Waterval Onder there was a steep descent that the locomotive had to negotiate by means of a rack and pinion, and they ground their way down this at three or four miles an hour. Churchill was awakened in the morning by the banging and jerking of the train as the engine was again coupled to the trucks at Waterval Onder. Here Burnham went into the village for food and drink, and was told by the hotel owner that Winston Churchill had passed through two days before dressed as a Roman Catholic priest. They reached Kaapmuiden, a small farming town, the following morning. The station was swarming with armed Boers, but the train chugged off again without incident.

The train rattled on through the Transvaal landscape, and late in the afternoon they reached Komatipoort, lying at the confluence of the Crocodile and Komati rivers and near the border between the Transvaal and Portuguese

A NZASM locomotive creeping uphill towards Waterval-Boven

The small town of Waterval Boven, *circa* 1900. The station is the fourth building from left

Nooitgedacht Station

East Africa. Peeping through the chink, Churchill could see that it was a busy place, with numerous trains and large numbers of people moving about. As the train pulled up, he covered himself with a piece of sacking and lay flat on the floor of the wagon. The cross-border trains were always thoroughly searched, but fortunately, through Burnham's connections with the chief detective, one Morris, the wool was to be transported straight through to Lourenço Marques. Nevertheless, the train was not cleared to go through into Portuguese territory until eleven o'clock the next morning.

Eventually darkness set in and again Churchill was concerned about the risk of snoring, but in the end he slept without incident. When he woke, the train was still stationary and he worried that the delay had been caused by the train being thoroughly searched. He was also anxious that they had been forgotten on the siding and might be left there for days or even weeks. But by eleven o'clock they were coupled and almost immediately steamed off. As the train crossed the long iron bridge over the Komati River, Churchill finally found himself in Portuguese territory.

A German volunteer, Franco Seiner, who had travelled from Lourenço

The Komati River bridge with the Lebombo Mountains in the distance, 1900

Marques to Pretoria to join the Boers, described the landscape beyond the Transvaal border as 'immeasurable flats of swamps on either side of the railway line, only partially grown with high reeds, orchids and various tropical plants. Except for a few coconut palms only the so-called fever-tree (*koortsboom*) [is] present. Often we also saw native huts, of which the inhabitants were doing duty as railway guards.'[4] From here on, before reaching Lourenço Marques, the palm trees, aloes and cacti became more abundant.

When the train arrived at the next station, Churchill saw the caps of the Portuguese officials on the platform and the name Resana Garcia painted on a board. As the train moved on again, he was so overcome with joy and relief that he pushed his head out of the tarpaulin, sang, shouted and fired two or three gunshots into the air as an expression of joy. In the late afternoon, the train reached Lourenço Marques and stopped in a goods yard where a crowd of black railway workers came to unload it.

The moment had now come to leave his hiding place. He slipped out from the end of the wagon between the couplings and mingled unnoticed with the blacks and loafers in the yard, which was probably not difficult in his dirty,

View of Lourenço Marques and Delagoa Bay at the end of the nineteenth century

unkempt state. He then strolled towards the station exit and soon found himself in the streets of the city. Outside the station, Burnham – who had been obliged to board a passenger train at Resana Garcia – was waiting for him. Burnham walked off into the town with Churchill following some twenty yards behind. They passed through several streets and turned a number of corners. Then Burnham stopped and looked up towards the roof of a building on the opposite side of the street. Churchill followed his gaze and saw the Union Jack fluttering above the British Consulate.

At first, the secretary to the British consul told him at the door that the consul could not see him that day, and that he had to come back the next day. With his scruffy appearance, Churchill must have made a poor impression. But this reception riled him, and he made such a fuss that the consul himself finally came to the door. And soon Churchill could enjoy a hot bath, clean clothing and a good dinner. From the newspapers he learnt that a 'black week' had struck the British Army – General Gatacre at Stormberg, Lord Methuen at Magersfontein and Sir Redvers Buller at Colenso had all suffered defeats, with the most casualties sustained by England since the Crimean War. Churchill now became eager to rejoin the soldiers at the Natal front.

Lourenço Marques was full of Boers and their sympathisers. Fortunately, however, the weekly steamer was leaving for Durban the following day. Concerned that the Boers in the Portuguese colony might try to recapture Churchill, a party of armed Britons escorted him to the docks and onto the steamer. He sailed on board the *Induna* from Delagoa Bay to Durban. It was a smooth journey, and on the afternoon of 23 December, Churchill arrived in Durban, where more than twenty large transport and supply vessels lay at anchor. Three others carrying soldiers were waiting for pilots to take them into the harbour.

On reaching the jetty, he saw that a large cheering crowd had gathered, and he came to realise that he was the object of this big welcome. Bands were playing on the dock-

Churchill after his escape

side and flags and bunting fluttered in the breeze. Churchill was hoisted onto their shoulders and deposited on the steps of the old town hall.[5] The people demanded a speech, and Churchill ably obliged with some well-chosen words. This took place at the intersection of West[6] and Church streets, and there is still a plaque marking the spot where Churchill made his address.

After an hour of hero worship, which Churchill admitted he thoroughly enjoyed, he made his way to the evening train bound for Pietermaritzburg. The train journey passed very quickly with the aid of a month's newspapers to read.

In spite of his glorious reception in Durban, not everyone shared the adulation for Churchill that swept the country and Britain. The Durban news-

Churchill making his speech in Durban after his escape

paper the *Phoenix* had published an article while Churchill was in prison, stating that although hoping he would not be shot by the Transvaal authorities, 'at the same time the Boer General [Piet Joubert] cannot be blamed should he order his execution'.[7] Both *Blackwood's Magazine* and the *Daily Nation* accused Churchill of having been dishonourable by breaking his parole. Among others, the influential *Westminster Gazette* reported that 'we hardly understand the application which Mr Churchill is reported to have made to General Joubert asking to be released on the ground that he was a newspaper correspondent and had taken "no part in the fighting"'.[8] Hinting at the fact that Churchill could not play hero during the war – which he hoped would be publicly reported to enhance his career – and at the same time claim to be merely a correspondent, the *Westminster Gazette* stated that he 'cannot have the best of both worlds'.[9]

What also counted against the escapee was Captain Haldane's claim that he had been left in the lurch by Churchill, who used Haldane's plan and then compromised his and Brockie's chances of escaping.[10] Haldane, in fact, later made an even more daring escape by tunnelling out of the prison, but this never received the kind of publicity Churchill enjoyed.

It has to be borne in mind that Churchill's escape coincided with a time

The Churchill commemorative plaque in Durban

that the war was going badly for Britain – humiliating defeats at Magersfontein, Stormberg and Colenso – and the depressed nation needed a hero in their darkest hour. So when Winston Churchill made his daring escape, the British press and public leapt at the incident to create that hero. And Churchill being Churchill knew just how to exploit the opportunity.

8

Colenso and Spioen Kop

'The shells were falling on the hill from both sides, as I counted, at the
rate of seven a minute, and the strange discharges of the Maxim shell
guns lacerated the hillsides with dotted chains of smoke and dust.
A thick and continual stream of wounded flowed rearwards.
A village of ambulance wagons grew up at the foot of the mountain.
The dead and injured, smashed and broken by the shells, littered
the summit till it was a bloody, reeking shambles.'[1]

HAVING ARRIVED IN PIETERMARITZBURG, Churchill rested for a
day at Government House and had conversations with the governor of
Natal, Sir Walter Hely-Hutchinson, and the prime minister of the colony,
William Philip Schreiner, who, according to Churchill, talked only of the
importance of fighting the war to the end. In the past, Government House
had hosted many famous visitors like Voortrekker Andries Pretorius, President
Paul Kruger and local notables, including Bishop Colenso.[2] Churchill also
found time to visit the hospitals, housed in barracks, which before the war
had been occupied by soldiers. He was met by the grim sight of wounded
and maimed soldiers, and left the places with a sense of relief. Eager to get
to the Natal front, he took the night mail train north to the British camp at
Frere. Private Tucker wrote from here in his diary that on Christmas Eve at
nine o'clock in the evening, a typical South African thunderstorm struck and
continued all night.[3] Churchill arrived at Frere at dawn on Christmas Day.

Here General Buller was still trying to repel the Boers' siege of Ladysmith,
smarting from the mid-December defeat at Colenso. The Siege of Ladysmith
had begun on 2 November 1899 and would last for almost four months,
until 28 February 1900. Before the siege, the Boers had had big successes at

Government House, a well-known national monument in Pietermaritzburg

Modderspruit and Nicholson's Nek on 30 October, where the British suffered heavy casualties: 203 dead and wounded, and 817 captured – the biggest loss of British troops since the Napoleonic Wars. Buller first established his headquarters at Frere and then at Chieveley. On 15 December, three days after Churchill's escape from Pretoria, he had tried unsuccessfully to break through at Colenso by attacking General Louis Botha's force.

When Churchill rejoined Buller's forces, he noticed that in his absence things had changed significantly. Along the hills, where Boer riflemen had been shooting for some time, British pickets were now posted, and in the valley in which the British had lain exposed to their artillery fire now stood the white tents of a large army. The iron bridge across the Blue Krantz River lay wrecked at the bottom of the ravine and had been replaced by a substantial wooden structure, and all along the line near the station new sidings had been built. But the Boers were still holding Colenso and still besieging Ladysmith.

Back at Chieveley, Churchill took up quarters in a plate-layer's hut within a hundred yards of the spot where he had been taken prisoner a little more than a month before. He was also reunited with his valet, Thomas Walden. When he met Buller, the general was naturally in poor spirits after his defeat at Colenso. Buller nevertheless was pleased to see the young man, and wrote to a friend: 'Winston Churchill turned up here yesterday escaped from Pretoria.

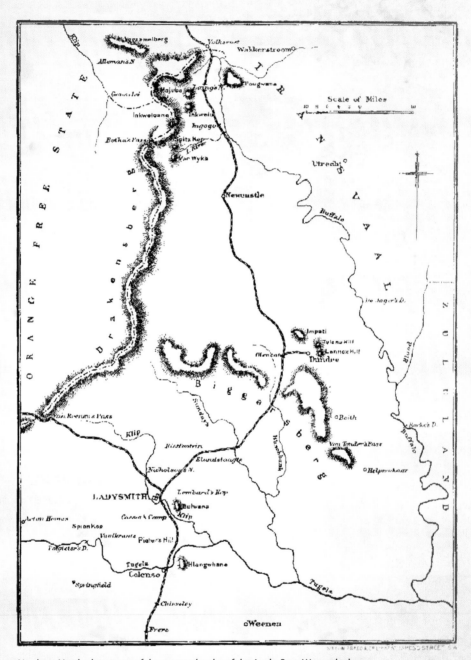

Northern Natal, where some of the greatest battles of the Anglo-Boer War took place

The British camp at Chieveley, where Churchill rejoined General Buller's troops

He really is a fine fellow and I must say I admire him greatly. I wish he was leading irregular troops instead of writing for a rotten paper. We are very short of good men.'[4] Churchill repeated Buller's wish for more men in a dispatch to the *Morning Post*, questioning whether the English gentlemen were too busy fox hunting, which of course did not go down well in England.

Charles Burne of the Naval Brigade recorded that on New Year's Day 1900, after 'a fine bowl of punch, with slices of pine-apple in it' at midnight, they shelled the Boers and that 'Winston Churchill came up to look at our firing'. And on 6 January, Burne wrote: 'We have Bennet Burleigh, Winston Churchill, Hubert of *The Times*, and many others, constantly on Gun Hill looking at our firing.'[5]

Churchill told Buller that he would like to observe more of the fighting, but that he had to continue sending dispatches to the *Morning Post*. To his delight, Buller gave him a lieutenancy in the South African Light Horse without requiring him to cease his job as war correspondent, prompting Churchill to remark to his mother that he was 'evidently… in very high favour'.[6] So, on 2 January 1900, Churchill joined the Cockyoli Birds, so called after the feathers of the sakabula bird they wore in their slouch hats.

Churchill in the SA Light Horse uniform, showing the sakabula bird feathers in his slouch hat – hence their nickname, the Cockyoli Birds

Lady Randolph Churchill with her son John as a patient on the hospital ship *Maine*

At the same time, Churchill seized the opportunity to ask for a lieutenancy for his brother, John, in the same regiment. John had in the meantime left his job in London and sailed for South Africa as a volunteer. The request was granted by Buller.

Soon afterwards their mother would also find herself in South Africa. On 28 January 1900, she arrived in Durban on board the hospital ship *Maine*, which had been purchased for £40 000 by a group of Anglo-Americans. She was to manage the medical activities on the ship. Ironically, one of her first patients was John, who was wounded in the leg on 12 February near Hussar Hill while involved in the same action as his brother. 'Lady Randolph Churchill superintended all the arrangements for the reception of the men on board the *Maine*, and personally directed the berthing,' reported *The Nursing Record & Hospital World*. 'Lady Randolph was here, there, and everywhere, flitting about amongst the invalids like a "ministering angel".'[7]

In the meantime, on 6 January 1900, the Boers had made a determined effort to capture the besieged Lady-smith by attacking Wagon Hill, which was heavily defended by the British. A *Times* correspondent wrote:

> Ladysmith does not lend itself readily to defence. Roughly, the town lies in the bend of a horseshoe. But the hills which make this formation are disconnected, and the ranges and spurs straggle over a large area. Not only are they uneven, but their continuations stretch away in every direction, and form positions which in the majority of cases actually command the town. With the force at his [General White's] disposal it was, of course, impossible to hold every hill.[8]

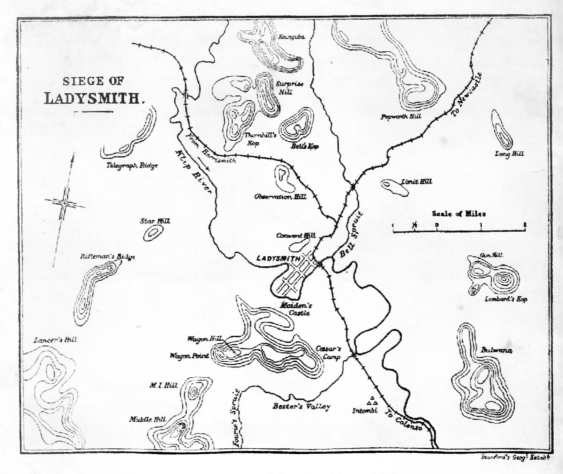

SIEGE OF
LADYSMITH.

Nanquba

Surprise Hill

Thornhill's Kop

Bell's Kop

Pepworth Hill

To Newcastle

Long Hill

Telegraph Ridge

Klip River

From Harrismith

Observation Hill

Limit Hill

Scale of Miles

Star Hill

Convent Hill

Bell Spruit

Rifleman's Ridge

LADYSMITH

Gun Hill

Lombard's Kop

Maiden's Castle

Lancer's Hill

Wagon Hill

Wagon Point

Cæsar's Camp

Bulwana

M I Hill

Fowrie's Spruit

Middle Hill

Bester's Valley

Intombi

To Colenso

Stanford's Geogl Estabt

Wagon Hill was a key position, and once it fell Ladysmith would lie open. But the Boers suffered heavy losses. Eighteen miles away at their camp at Chieveley, Churchill and the men were very much aware of the fighting, listening to the sound of gunfire. At daybreak an officer came to his tent, suggesting that something big was happening at Ladysmith, which was confirmed by the fact that until 10:30 a.m. there had not been the slightest let-off in the bombardments. Later, however, they gradually died away. At about noon, a heliograph message arrived, saying that there had been a general attack on all sides by the Boers, which was repulsed all round, but that the fighting was still going on.

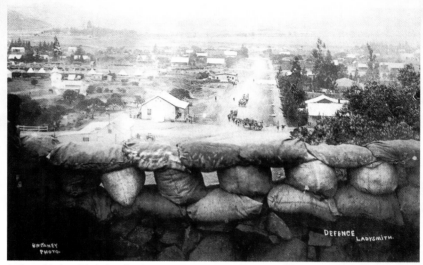

A view of Ladysmith during the siege

On the same day, at lunchtime at Chieveley, Churchill and the men received the order for the whole force to make a demonstration before Colenso with the object of luring some of the Boers back from Ladysmith to hopefully relieve the pressure on Sir George White. Besides creating this diversion, they were also hoping that the Boers would reveal their positions, especially those of their guns. But in the latter respect, they failed because the Boers declined to be drawn. As Churchill remarked, it needed a patient man to beat a Dutchman at waiting.

Back at the camp they heard that at Ladysmith the Boers had begun a general attack on the outposts around the town, focusing their efforts on Caesar's Camp and Wagon Hill, but had been repulsed with heavy losses. They also learnt that Sir Charles Warren's division was to march to Frere the same day, and when Churchill rode from Chieveley to Frere on the afternoon of 10 January, he found the whole of General Warren's division already at the Frere camp.

General Buller now moved his headquarters to Springfield (now Winterton) on the Upper Tugela River, where by mid-January he had gathered 24 000 men and fifty-eight cannons. He planned his offensive to commence

Remains of Caesar's Camp defences on Wagon Hill, showing Ladysmith in the background

Remains of the Manchesters' fort, Caesar's Camp

The British memorial at Caesar's Camp

A crude Boer gravestone, displayed on Wagon Hill

Typical grassland on the Tugela front

on 20 January 1900, on two fronts. Given command of 15 000 men, General Warren was ordered to attempt to outflank the Boers under General Botha by crossing the Tugela River, while Buller and his troops were to break through the hills lower down. Churchill was a member of one of four cavalry squadrons of the South African Light Horse, commanded by Douglas Cochrane, 12th Earl of Dundonald.

The scenario was that the Boers had established themselves in almost impregnable positions north of the Tugela, among ranges of high hills littered with boulders and trees. At the bottom of these hills, the river flowed rapidly, and on the opposite (British) side, lay undulating, grassy terrain. Boer numbers ranged from 12 000 (according to Churchill's information from Pretoria) to 15 000 (according to the Intelligence Branch) and they were armed with the best magazine rifles, and supported by fifteen to twenty quick-firing guns. The drifts of the Tugela, which the British columns had to cross, were all surrounded by trenches, and once through, the British still faced some twenty miles of broken country of ridge after ridge.

British troops on the Natal front

The cavalry, in which Churchill served as an officer, was responsible for the safety of the baggage convoy, and Churchill was frustrated by the vast amount of material the army was carting along, which badly hampered its movements. There were ox wagons, mule wagons, Scotch carts, ambulance wagons, ammunition carts, artillery, slaughter cattle and finally the naval battery drawn by long strings of animals. He lamented the fact that every private soldier had his own canvas shelter, and he had never before experienced officers accommodated with tents on service, even though both the Indian frontier and the Sudan were hotter than South Africa. He concluded that it was poor economy to let a soldier live well for three days at the price of killing him on the fourth.

Churchill described the Natal landscape as they rode:

So on we ride, trot and walk, lightly and easily over the good turf, and winding in scattered practical formations among the beautiful verdant hills of Natal. Presently we topped a ridge and entered a very extensive basin of country – a huge circular valley of green grass with sloping hills apparently on all sides and towards the west, bluffs, rising range above range, to the bright purple wall of the Drakensberg. Other valleys opened out from this, some half veiled in thin mist, others into which the sun was shining, filled with a curious blue light, so that one seemed to be looking down into depths of clear water, and everyone rejoiced in the splendours of the delightful landscape.[9]

The troops reached Springfield without incident, and there were no Boers to be seen anywhere. Springfield consisted of three houses, a long wooden bridge, and half a dozen farms with tin roofs. Clumps of trees could be seen in the neighbourhood. Churchill went to the village store, where he was served by one Anna Beyers, whose daughter, Lettie Bennet, many years later had an amusing story to tell about Churchill's visit to the shop: 'He trotted up the dusty lane and tethered his horse outside the shop. He bought candlesticks and sardines. My mother told me how she could never forget the way he lisped when he asked for the sardines ... Mr Churchill then looked around and spotted the chickens in the yard. He asked if he could buy one, to which my mother replied, "Yes, if you can catch it."'[10] So Churchill had to chase the chickens around in the yard, probably not too gracefully, until he finally caught one. Then he rode off with the candlesticks, sardines and a chicken.

Anna Beyers, who served Churchill in her uncle's shop at Springfield, where he chased after the chickens

After a while, the troops had all crossed the wooden bridge and watered their horses in the Little Tugela, which was swollen by the rains to some eighty yards wide. Three hundred men and two guns were left to hold the Springfield bridge, while 700 men and four guns hurried on to the heights commanding the town of Potgieter's Ferry. They reached it safely by late afternoon, and found an unoccupied strong position strengthened by loopholed stone walls. The whole force climbed to the top of the hills, dragging the guns with them. From their lofty position they commanded a good view of the whole country

The Drakensberg dominates the Natal skyline

beyond the Tugela. The ground dropped 600 feet almost sheer to the bottom of the valley, where the Tugela twisted and turned. In a big loop of the river they could see the ferry moored to ropes. The ford beside it was closed at the time due to the flood.

Once all his forces had crossed the river, Warren sent part of an infantry division under Lieutenant General Sir Francis Clery against the Boer right flank occupying positions on a plateau named Tabanyama. But the Boers had entrenched a new position on the reverse slopes of the plateau, and Clery's attack made no progress. At Tabanyama two Dutchmen, Henri Slegtkamp and Albert de Roos, and a Scot, the well-known Jack Hindon (who later commanded a scouting corps), made a name for themselves. At some stage during the battle, following heavy artillery and rifle fire, the burghers decided to abandon the ridge, but the three men climbed up the hill under heavy fire and against the tide of retreating Boers. From here, under a raised federal flag, they kept up such relentless fire that the Khakis were under the impression that the position was still manned by a large number of Boers.

Churchill wrote that he had seen many dead men in his time, at Omdurman and elsewhere, but that witnessing the Boer dead had aroused the most painful emotions. He mentioned a field cornet of Heilbron, De Mentz, a grey-haired man of over sixty, whose stony face still showed resolve in death. Boer prisoners later told him that De Mentz had refused all suggestions of surrender, and bleeding profusely from a heavily injured leg, continued to fire until he bled to death. Beside him lay a boy of about seventeen, shot through the heart, and further on lay two British riflemen with their heads in pieces like eggshells.

The bloodiest battle of the war was still to come, however. North-east of General Warren's force lay Spioen Kop, the largest hill in the region, almost at the centre of the Boer lines. If the British could capture this position and bring artillery to the hill, they would command the flanks of the surrounding Boer positions.

On the night of 23 January, Warren sent the larger part of his force under

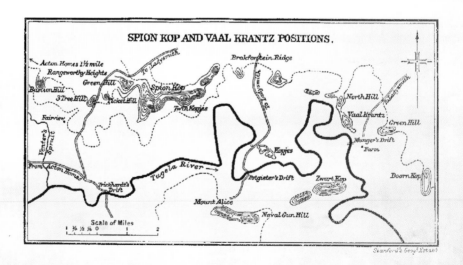

Boer council of war prior to the Battle of Spioen Kop. General Louis Botha is seated in the dark clothes

Major General Edward Woodgate to secure Spioen Kop. Lieutenant Colonel Alexander Thorneycroft was selected to lead the initial assault. The British climbed the hill at night and in dense mist surprised the small Boer picket and drove them off. A half-company of British sappers began to entrench the position, and Woodgate notified Warren of the successful capture of the hilltop. As soon as the news spread through the camps that the British troops were occupying the top of Spioen Kop, Churchill hurried to Gun Hill, where the batteries were arrayed, and he watched the battle from a flank.

On the Boer side, General Louis Botha sent for reinforcements from as far as Acton Homes, Vaalkrantz and the Boer laagers around Ladysmith, then mustered his men. By seven o'clock in the morning, the Boers held Aloe Knoll and Green Hill, while the right wing of the Carolina commando hid behind the crest of Spioen Kop, hardly 200 yards from the enemy. As dawn broke, the British discovered that they held only the smaller and lower part of the hilltop of Spioen Kop, while the Boers occupied higher ground on three sides of their position. The British infantry in the trenches could not see over the crest of the plateau, and the Boers were able to fire down the length of

Wounded are taken from Spioen Kop

the trenches from Green Hill, Aloe Knoll and Conical Hill. In the battle for the crest that followed, the fiercest of the Boer War, both sides suffered dreadful casualties.

Churchill witnessed the carnage from the British camp. He counted the shells falling on the hill from both sides at the rate of seven a minute, with the result that a continuous stream of wounded was moved towards the rear. At the foot of the mountain the number of ambulance wagons grew rapidly. On the summit lay many dead and wounded. The Dorset Regiment was ordered to support the struggling troops and then the Scottish Rifles and the 3rd King's Royal Rifles from Potgieter's Ferry. As night closed in, the British were still in possession of the hill.

At about four o'clock in the morning, Churchill rode with Captain R. Brooke of the 7th Hussars to Spioen Kop to ascertain the situation. They passed through the ambulance village, left their horses behind and climbed up the spur. Along the way, they encountered streams of wounded, either struggling along on their own, or supported by comrades or carried on stretchers. Here and there they saw corpses. Fighting was still proceeding, and only the Dorset Regiment had not yet been thrown into the battle. Churchill

The terrible British casualties in the main trench at Spioen Kop, the day after the battle

The same trench today, taken from just off to the right

Top: The main British trench at Spioen Kop today; Middle:
View from the ridge of Spioen Kop; Bottom: Memorial in
remembrance of the Boers who died on Spioen Kop

The position of an old Boer trench marked out on Spioen Kop

and Brooke then returned to inform Sir Charles Warren, who had not yet received proper reports, about what they had seen. What seemed clear from the British point of view was that, unless sufficient cover could be gained during the night and guns dragged to the summit to counter the Boer artillery, the infantry would probably not last another day.

Warren wanted to be apprised of Colonel Thorneycroft's views of the situation, and Churchill was sent back for this purpose. He encountered more stragglers and wounded men, and little groups collected by officers, but in the darkness there was confusion. He found Colonel Thorneycroft sitting at the top of the mountain, surrounded by the remnants of the regiment he had raised. But by then the decision had already been taken: Thorneycroft had not received any messages from the general and, expecting no guns, he had decided to retreat. According to Churchill, he argued that six good battalions safely down the hill were better than a mop up in the morning.

Indian stretcher bearers on the battlefield

When the Boers realised the next morning that the British had abandoned their efforts, they reoccupied the hill.

An interesting fact is that there were three men present at Spioen Kop who were to become known the world over. One was an Indian stretcher bearer for the British Army by the name of Mohandas Gandhi,[11] destined to become the world-famous Indian pacifist; another was General Louis Botha, who would later become South Africa's first prime minister; and then there was, of course, Churchill himself.

The day before the attack on Spioen Kop, when Churchill was crossing the pontoon bridge, he had recognised one of his fellow

Mohandas Gandhi as a young man

pupils from Harrow School, a smart, clean-looking young gentleman, as he described him, who was riding with the Irregular Horse. He had just arrived in Natal and was on his way to the front. On the morning of 25 January, after the battle, Churchill was told that an 'unauthorised press correspondent' had been found among the dead on the summit of Spioen Kop, killed by a gun shell, and found leaning forward on his rifle with a pair of shattered field glasses bearing his name. The dead soldier turned out to be his old school mate M'Corquodale, whom he had met the day before.

9

Tugela Heights and the relief of Ladysmith

*'Those who live under the conditions of a civilised city, who lie
abed till nine and ten of the clock in artificially darkened rooms,
gain luxury at the expense of joy. But the soldier, who fares simply,
sleeps soundly, and rises with the morning star, wakes in an elation
of body and spirit without an effort and with scarcely a yawn.
There is no more delicious moment in the day than this, when
we light the fire and, while the kettle boils, watch the dark
shadows of the hills take form, perspective, and finally colour,
knowing that there is another whole day begun, bright
with chance and interest, and free from all cares.'[1]*

AFTER THE EVACUATION OF SPIOEN KOP, the British troops made
their retreat on the night of 26 January in driving rain and pitched
camp at Spearman's Hill. General Buller tried his best to motivate the troops,
promising that they would be in Ladysmith soon. He would make his third
attempt to lift the siege on 5 February at Vaalkrantz. During this time, Churchill
was experiencing to the full his dual role as soldier and correspondent. The
day before the Battle of Vaalkrantz, he wrote from Spearman's Hill about the
joys of being a soldier out in the veld, rising with the morning star and watching the landscape unfold in the first rays of daylight while the kettle is boiling.

The next few days, however, only brought disappointment. Between Spioen
Kop and Doornkloof mountain lay a low ridge known as Brakfontein, with
a detached hill called Vaalkrantz. Buller's plan was to take Vaalkrantz and
pass his troops through on the plateau beyond. By nightfall on 5 February,
the whole of General Lyttelton's brigade had occupied Vaalkrantz and were

Wounded troops are ferried across the Tugela River

entrenching themselves. But after three days of skirmishing, Buller found that his position was so cramped that there was no room to drag his superior artillery up to support the British infantry, and on 8 February, the general retirement of the army to Springfield and Spearman's Hill was in full swing.

An interesting fact is that some Boer *agterryers* (outriders) apparently participated with the burghers of Commandant Ben Viljoen (later to become general) in the battle at Vaalkrantz. Lieutenant Lambton of the Durham Light Infantry reported that on cresting the hill, they saw a group of at least six black men, armed with rifles and wearing bandoliers. Lambton was wounded by one of them. Churchill also commented on the incident, writing that among those Boers who remained to fight to the end were five or six armed black men, and that the Boers evidently had no scruples in employing blacks to fight with them.[2] Throughout the war, the Boers insisted that they never armed blacks or had them take part in battles, but their claim seems to have been false.[3]

The mortal remains of the British soldiers whose graves were on the left bank of the Tugela and on Vaalkrantz have been exhumed and reinterred in

Crossing the Tugela

the Vaalkrantz Garden of Remembrance, near the foot of the hill. The names of those who were killed or died of wounds and buried at Vaalkrantz, Spearman's Farm (now Mount Alice Farm) and Mooi River are inscribed on a large British monument in the garden. A memorial to Major Johnson-Smyth, killed while leading the 68th Regiment Durham Light Infantry, has also been moved from the bank of the river to this site. Of the Boers buried at Vaalkrantz, the graves of eight were exhumed and their remains transferred to the Burgher Monument at Ladysmith, which displays the names of thirty-nine Boers who fell at Vaalkrantz. The graves of thirty-one men of the Johannesburg, Krugersdorp and Standerton commandos have not been located. Several stone walls and gun emplacements built by the Boers and Khakis at the time of the battle can still be seen on Vaalkrantz and Kranskloof.

On 12 February, Buller ordered a fourth attempt, hoping to exploit his ten-to-one superiority in artillery and four-to-one advantage in numbers.

Two British soldiers having a meal during the Natal campaign

His offensive would become known as the Battle of Tugela Heights and would last from 12 to 27 February.

Churchill was involved in a reconnaissance of Hussar Hill, the high ground opposite Hlangwane and the ridges of Monte Cristo and Cingolo, on which the British artillery had been positioned to prepare for the attack. 'It was the point where the open veldt ceased and the bush country began,' explained a *Times* correspondent. 'In front lay the thickly wooded valley of the Gomba Spruit, a small stream running eastward from Hlangwane Hill, and to the south lies the equally bushy Blaauwkrantz Valley. The bush consists chiefly of stunted mimosa and is intersected by innumerable dongas, so, though it forms excellent cover for troops, their advance is necessarily very slow.'[4]

During this operation, Churchill's brother, John, was wounded and had to go to hospital. Winston happened to pass along the line when he saw John being hit, and discovered that he had been shot through the leg. Although

Bontebok roaming the veld above the Tugela

the wound was not serious, the doctors said that he would need to spend a month in hospital. Therefore John ended up on the hospital ship *Maine* in Durban, where his mother was tending to the British wounded.[5]

On 14 February, the British conquered Hussar Hill; Cingolo Hill, to the north-east of Hussar Hill, was next to fall. The terrain they had to pass through to the hill was difficult, with rock, high grass and dense thickets, so the troops, including Churchill, had to dismount and lead their horses on foot. The Boers on the hill were outnumbered and fell back, and the British took the top of the hill. Then on 18 February, the British took the 1 000-foot-high Monte Cristo and cleared Green Hill. As soon as Monte Cristo was taken, Churchill telegraphed to the *Morning Post* that now at last success was a distinct possibility, as it had laid open a practicable road to Ladysmith.[6]

The outflanked Boers abandoned Hlangwane and the south bank entirely on 19 February, and in the afternoon Hart's brigade advanced from Chieveley,

The bushy area around Cingolo Hill

and his leading battalion occupied Colenso village without any resistance. The railhead was advanced to Colenso Station, and on 21 February the British Army began to cross the river. On 22 February, they captured the Boer positions at Horseshoe Hill and Wynne's Hill, north of Colenso. The following day, they attacked Hart's Hill, where the Royal Inniskilling Fusiliers, especially, suffered heavy casualties, but fortunately for Buller, two battalions of reinforcements arrived in time to prevent a rout.

Buller began to look for another way to flank the Boers: they would strike at the Boers' left flank, first at Pieter's Hill, then Railway Hill and finally at Hart's Hill. At the same time, another division would threaten the Boers' centre and right flanks.

Pieter's Hill was attacked on 27 February – the anniversary of the Boers' famous victory in the Battle of Majuba in 1881 – but as Botha reinforced his threatened flank, the assault stalled. The British, however, took the saddle

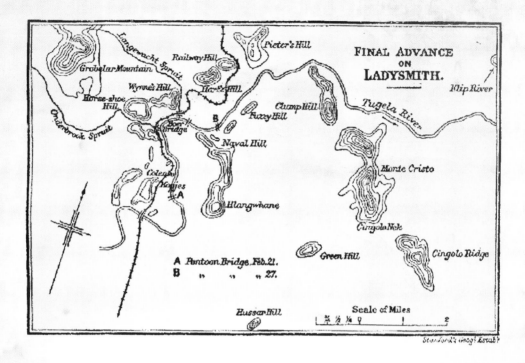

between Hart's Hill and Railway Hill, and then began their assault on Hart's Hill. A sustained charge cleared the crest, forcing Botha's men to fall back from the heights. On 28 February, the great column of Boer horsemen and wagons moved rapidly north, and eventually the Boers under General Botha retreated through the Drakensberg into the Transvaal Highveld after riding north through the bushveld. They continued guerrilla operations in the eastern Transvaal, while a second force under General Ben Viljoen operated in the north-east around Lydenburg.

In the afternoon of 28 February 1900, two squadrons of mounted infantry – the Natal Carbineers and the Imperial Light Horse – under Major Hubert Gough of the 16th Lancers rode into Ladysmith, thus ending the siege. The people of Ladysmith, who numbered over 21000, were overjoyed, civilians and military alike – for 118 days they had suffered the ravages of disease and starvation, and had been continually shelled by the Boers. So Gough and his troops rode into a jubilant heroes' welcome.

Churchill, however, had to wait a while before entering Ladysmith because

The terrain of Pieter's Hill, with Aasvoëlkop on the left in the distance and Monte Cristo to the right

An old Boer trench facing Railway Hill is marked out

HERE REST THREE OFFICERS AND THIRTEEN MEN OF THE SOMERSET LIGHT INFANTRY AND AN OFFICER OF THE ROYAL ARMY MEDICAL CORPS WHO WERE KILLED IN ACTION ON THE COLENSO KOPJES ON 21st FEBRUARY 1900

A memorial to officers and troopers killed on the Colenso koppies

Hart's Hill on the Tugela Heights

Railway Hill, which fell to the British on 27 February 1900

it was not until evening that two squadrons of the South African Light Horse were allowed to ride through to the town. He recalled:

> Never shall I forget that ride. The evening was deliciously cool. My horse was strong and fresh, for I had changed him at midday. The ground was rough with many stones, but we cared little for that. Beyond the next ridge, or the rise beyond that, or around the corner of the hill, was Ladysmith – the goal of all our hopes and ambitions during weeks of almost ceaseless fighting. Ladysmith – the centre of the world's attention, the scene of famous deeds, the cause of mighty efforts – Ladysmith was within our reach at last. We were going to be inside the town within an hour. The excitement of the moment was increased by the exhilaration of the gallop. Onward wildly, recklessly, up and down hill, over the boulders, through the scrub, Hubert Gough with his two squadrons, McKenzie's Natal Carbineers and the Imperial Light Horse, were clear of the ridges already. We turned the shoulder of a hill, and there before us lay the tin houses and dark trees we had come so far to see and save.[7]

Memorial on the Tugela Heights to the
Imperial soldiers who lost their lives
between 22 and 27 February 1900

Lionel James, a correspondent with *The Times*, was on the scene when Major Gough entered Ladysmith and disputes Churchill's claim that he was the first. 'Neither Churchill or Dundonald were at the Drift nor were they at White's HQ,' he said.[8] At about five o'clock in the evening, Major Gough and Major McKenzie, with a section of the Natal Carbineers, crossed the drift where the Ladysmith Natal Carbineers had their camp and Sir George White met them.

James was ready to depart for Ladysmith immediately with his 'scoop' and approached General White for permission and a pass, which was granted. White asked James to go straight to Buller on Pieter's Hill with a request to send the cavalry after the Boers, who were retreating towards Modderspruit. On reaching Buller, James handed him the message. It appears that his report appeared in *The Times* in London the following morning. James saw that Buller was not making any effort to follow White's suggestion, to which Buller replied that 'he did not consider Ladysmith to have been relieved until his [Buller's] men signalled to this effect from the top of Umbulwabe'. He did, however, agree to send James's report to *The Times* as soon as he could. Churchill arrived at Buller's headquarters on 1 March, requesting that, as he had been the first into Ladysmith, it should be his dispatches that were to be sent first. But Buller stood by his agreement with James.

On the night that the first troops arrived in Ladysmith, Churchill dined with the headquarters staff, including Ian Hamilton, and special reserve bottles of champagne were uncorked. Churchill wrote that he had expected to be served horse flesh, but that the last ox was slaughtered in honour of the occasion.[9] The dinner, hosted by General White, was held at the house of the Christopher family, named Budleigh. Set in large, park-like gardens, this old colonial-style house, with its wide verandahs, is today still one of the proud historical gems of Ladysmith.

Sir Ian Hamilton

British troops enter Ladysmith, ending the Boer siege of the town

Grand as this may sound, American war correspondent Richard Harding Davis in *With Both Armies in South Africa*, paints a rather depressing picture of the town nevertheless:

> The town itself did not arouse one's sympathies. It straggles for a mile on either side of a wide dusty street. It consists of stone and corrugated-zinc shops of one story, a bare parade-ground, a court-house with a shattered bell-tower, and houses, also of one story and balanced by broad verandahs, set back in gardens yellow with dust. It is an unlovely, un-homelike place, set when it rains in a swamp of mud, and when the sun shines smothered in a plague of dust … For a whole morning at a time, when the wind sweeps down the street, Ladysmith's main avenue is a choking yellow fog, through which you can see but twenty feet about you.[10]

British troops marching through Ladysmith

On 3 March, the relieving army made a triumphant entry into Ladysmith and passed through the town to pitch camp on the plain beyond. The streets were lined with soldiers in their best clothes, and before the town hall – with its battered tower – sat Sir George White and his staff on their skinny horses with the pipers of the Gordon Highlanders opposite them. The townsfolk, by now hollow-eyed but jubilant, were crowding pavements and windows, and the bright colours of the Union Jack could be seen everywhere. At eleven o'clock, the relieving army began to march into the town, led by Sir Redvers Buller, his headquarters staff and an escort of the Royal Dragoons. All through the morning and into the afternoon, weary, dirty and tattered men flowed through the streets of Ladysmith. Harding Davis wrote that the men of the garrison were in clean khaki, pipe-clayed and brushed and polished, but their tunics hung on them as loosely as the flag around its pole. The skin on their cheek-bones was as tight and as yellow as the belly of a drum, their teeth protruded through parched, cracked lips, and hunger, fever, and suffering stared from out their eyes … In comparison the relieving column looked like giants as they came in with a swinging swagger, their uniforms blackened with mud and sweat and blood-stains, their faces brilliantly crimsoned and blistered and tanned by the dust and sun. They made a picture of strength and health and aggressiveness. Perhaps the contrast was strongest when the battalion of the Devonshire that had been on foreign service passed the 'reserve' battalion which had come from England. The men of the two battalions had parted five years before in India and they met again in Ladysmith with the men of one battalion lining the streets, sick, hungry, and yellow and the others, who had been fighting six weeks to reach it, marching toward them, robust, red-faced, and cheering mightily. As they met they gave a shout of recognition, and the men broke ranks and ran forward calling each other by name, embracing, shaking hands, and punching each other in the back and shoulders. It was a sight that very few men watched unmoved.[11]

Churchill himself was overcome by these scenes: 'It was a procession of lions. And presently, when the two battalions of Devons met – both full of honours – and old friends breaking from the ranks gripped each other's hands and shouted, everyone was carried away, and I waved my feathered hat, and cheered and cheered until I could cheer no longer for joy that I had lived to see the day.'[12]

During the days that followed, the celebrations continued. Churchill ate a food hamper destined for Pamela Plowden's brother-in-law, Major Edgar Lafone, as Lafone was too ill in hospital to appreciate it. He also polished off a bottle of 1825 brandy his mother had sent him, and asked for more, as he preferred it to the 1865 vintage he had brought out with him. Churchill walked through the streets of Ladysmith, looking at the damage done by the Boer shells during the town's bombardment. As mentioned, the town hall's tower had been wrecked and several houses bore large holes in their walls.

Intombi Camp, where Churchill visited the wounded and sick

He also visited the hospital camp by Intombi Spruit, where some 2 000 sick and wounded were accommodated, haggard and hungry. Nearly a tenth of the whole garrison had in the meantime died of disease. Numerous crosses marking the graves of 600 men had sprung up behind the camp. One evening, he went to see Sir George White, with whom he had a long conversation about the events in Natal.[13]

At the time of the siege, there were several other British war correspondents around the town. Most of the British dailies had sent reporters to South Africa and among them were H.H. Pearse of the *Daily News*, Henry Nevinson of the *Daily Chronicle*, Churchill's friend Leo Amery of *The Times* and George Stevens of the *Daily Mail*. Communications during the war were by telephone, native runner, heliograph, balloon, bicycle, searchlight, telegraph and even pigeon. Interestingly, Lionel James sent three copies of all his reports out of Ladysmith by native runner and at least one of each got through to London. James's report on the retreat from Dundee left Ladysmith just before it was sealed off, and was the only correspondent report to reach his London offices.

The relief force made good use of the telegraph and remained in direct contact with the War Office in London. In Ladysmith, the telegraph and telephone could not be used to communicate outside the town after the Boers had cut the lines, but had proved invaluable by keeping General White in touch with his outlying posts, in particular during the Battle of Platrand.

After the relief of Ladysmith, Churchill went to spend a few leisurely days on the *Maine*, moored in Durban, where his mother was looking after the British casualties. He visited the historic Durban Club, which had been founded before the Zulu Wars of 1879, and today still boasts Churchill as one of its illustrious visitors. Others include Prince Louis Napoleon, Thomas Baines, Sir Garnet Wolseley, generals Evelyn Wood and Redvers Buller, and lords Chelmsford, Roberts, Baden-Powell and Milner. Some famous men, including Churchill, are honoured by the club – two of the function rooms are named the Churchill Room and the Jan Smuts Room, and the main dining room is named after Lord Louis Mountbatten. There was a time when the waters of the bay came almost to the club's front boundary wall, but they have been separated to a great extent by reclamation.

After returning, Churchill spent about another month in Ladysmith. He invited his mother to see the town, and General Buller arranged passes for them. She had made a trip to Chieveley and Colenso earlier, and along the way saw the mangled wrecks of the derailed carriages left after the armoured-train ambush. After the relief of Ladysmith, Churchill could now accompany her. They met at Colenso and completed the leg into Ladysmith on an open trolley pushed by blacks, as there were no trains to the town at the time. Churchill pointed out the battlefields to his mother and told the stories surrounding them, which impressed her no end. As there was no hotel operating, they slept in the convent that served as Buller's headquarters. Lady Randolph then boarded a Red Cross train and returned to Durban, before sailing to England later in March.

At the time, Churchill read the first reviews of his only novel, *Savrola*, which concerns war and revolution. He had written it three years before while in Bangalore, and it was published in London and New York in February 1900. The novel contains scenes of fighting and bloodshed, which, given his experiences in the colonial wars, he would have had no problem portraying in words. He also decided to write a play set against the backdrop of the Anglo-Boer War, and asked his friend Pamela Plowden to approach the manager of

The Durban Club

Her Majesty's Theatre, Herbert Beerbohm Tree. But his mother put paid to the idea, claiming that the British public at the time would not be amenable to a war play.

While waiting in Ladysmith for the British campaign to get moving again, Churchill received a letter from an American agent, Major James Pond, offering to arrange a lecture tour of the United States, which would earn him a handy income as well as international fame. So by the end of 1900, and well before the end of the war, Churchill would be touring the United States, where he was to meet several famous Americans, including Mark Twain, President McKinley and Theodore Roosevelt.

10

Free State journey

'The town – a town of brick and tin – stands at the apparent edge of a vast plain of withered grass, from whose inhospitable aspect it turns and nestles, as if for protection, round the scrub-covered hills to northward. From among the crowd of one-storeyed dwelling-houses, more imposing structures … rise prominently to catch the eye and impress the mind with the pleasing prospect of wealthier civilisation.'[1]

W HILE CHURCHILL WAS IN NATAL, news arrived that Lord Roberts, advancing northwards from the Cape Colony into the Orange Free State, had relieved Kimberley, and surrounded and captured some 4000 Boers under General Piet Cronjé at Paardeberg. Cronjé's surrender on 27 February 1900 was a big blow to the Boer cause and a turning point in the war.

Lord Roberts, who took over command of the British forces from Sir Redvers Buller

Lord Roberts had been a great friend of Churchill's father, Lord Randolph Churchill. Winston had known Lord Roberts from his childhood days, and he therefore bargained on special treatment from the field marshal. But he was to discover that Roberts did not share the admiration or hero worship other people felt for him, and in fact had been quite upset about a report Churchill had written.

Because of their reverses, the Boers abandoned their invasion of Natal, withdrawing through the Drakensberg into their own territory. After Paardeberg, Lord Roberts advanced east towards Bloem-

British troops entering Bloemfontein, 13 March 1900

fontein, the Free State capital. General Christiaan de Wet and some 5 000 men were still active in the area, and at Modderrivierspoort he tried to stem the British tide, but the forces against him were overwhelming. More skirmishes followed at Poplar Grove and Abrahamskraal, but on 13 March, two weeks after Paardeberg, Bloemfontein was occupied unopposed. The poor British soldiers marching into the town were exhausted and dirty, and hardly looked like conquerors, but the loyalist citizens' enthusiasm was huge, and the men were greeted everywhere by British flags, rosettes and cheering. Lord Roberts occupied the Residency, while his soldiers set up camps to the west and south-west of the city.

Monument Hill from the Square, Bloemfontein, at the end of the nineteenth century

The view in the opposite direction, showing Upper Church Street

A correspondent for the *Bloemfontein Post* accompanying the troops described their entrance into the town:

> first past a few straggling shanties – poor shanties, but each with its
> bit of green garden patch – then past groups of little wooden houses,
> each with its narrow verandah and crinkled iron roof, then past
> continuous rows of houses, gradually enlarging as in a reversed
> perspective. And these began to have trees around and in front of
> them, and the trelliswork of their verandahs to grow more elaborately
> decorative. And women and girls – English-looking ladies in sailor hats
> and belts and blouses – were leaning over the verandah railings.[2]

In *From Aldershot to Pretoria: A Story of Christian Work Among Our Troops in South Africa*, W.E. Sellers – who had arrived with the troops with Roberts – wrote:

> It is a matter for thankfulness that the town was spared the horrors of a
> bombardment. It was far too beautiful to destroy. Of late years, as money
> had poured into the treasury, much had been expended upon public
> buildings. The Parliament Hall, for instance, had been erected at a cost
> of £80 000. The Grey College was a building of which any city might be
> proud. The Post Office was quite up to the average of some large
> provincial town in this country, and several other imposing buildings
> proved that the capital of the Orange Free State, though small, was 'no
> mean city'.
>
> It was literally a town on the veldt. The veldt was around it everywhere.
> It showed up now and then in the town where it was least expected, as
> though to assert its independence and remind the dwellers in the city
> that their fathers were its children.
>
> Wonderfully healthy is this little city. Situated high above sea level,
> with a climate so bracing and life-giving that the phthisis bacillus can
> hardly live in it, it seemed to our soldiers, after their long march across
> the veldt, a veritable City of Refuge.[3]

The historic Grey College, one of Bloemfontein's many attractive buildings, shortly before the Boer War

Impatient to get into the main theatre of the war, Churchill obtained an indefinite leave of absence from the South African Light Horse to transfer his activities as a correspondent to Lord Roberts's army, which at that time was occupying Bloemfontein, and the *Morning Post* made the necessary application for accreditation. He left the camp of Dundonald's brigade early in the morning of 29 March for the Ladysmith railway station and caught the ten o'clock morning train to Pietermaritzburg. The train reached the Intombi Spruit hospital camp in a quarter of an hour, but it was no longer there. Two days before, the last of the 2500 sick men had been moved to the hospital and convalescent camps at Mooi River and Highlands, or to the ships in Durban harbour. Nothing remained behind but tents and marquees, cookhouses, drinking-water tanks and the graves of the many who had perished during the previous months.

The train then sped across the well-known plain of Pieters, bringing back memories for Churchill of his slog across it as a captive casting longing eyes at the Ladysmith balloon. Then followed the deep ravine between Barton's Hill and Railway Hill, descending towards the Tugela along the front the Boers had formerly occupied – the slopes were still covered with little stone walls and traverses; white wooden crosses still marked the sites of the fallen. They crossed the temporary wooden bridge at Colenso into the open country beyond, past Gun Hill, and through the site of the Chieveley camp. Ironically, they also passed the wreck of the armoured train, still lying where Churchill and the other soldiers had moved it to clear the line, and on through Frere and Estcourt. After a seven-hour journey, they arrived in Pietermaritzburg.[4]

He had time for dinner in Pietermaritzburg before taking the night train to Durban, where he was fortunate to find a Union SS Company boat, the *Guelph*, leaving almost immediately for East London. (In *My Early Life*, Churchill wrote that he sailed to Port Elizabeth, but he actually disembarked in East London.) The weather was fine and the sea smooth, and after twenty-four hours they reached East London. From here he took the train towards Bloemfontein.

On his way to Ladysmith in November 1899, when he had taken the train from Cape Town via De Aar to East London, he travelled along the same route but in the opposite direction. This time, departing from East London, his first stop was Queenstown.[5] At the time, Queenstown was just outside the war zone, although martial law had been declared in the town. Its tree-lined streets radiated like the spokes of a wheel for defence purposes, a feature dating from the Border Wars, with lovely houses and gardens. Queenstown was predominantly English, a home away from home in the middle of the veld for the troops. Ladies with hats and parasols, parties on lawns, bands playing, rose gardens, croquet lawns and tennis courts imparted a British charm.

But Churchill did not get the chance to savour this atmosphere. At the station, passengers were only allowed a brief interval for refreshments, and he went to the dining room before they steamed off again towards Sterkstroom. Picturesquely situated among the foothills of the Stormberg range and over 1 300 metres above sea level, Sterkstroom was founded in 1875, and today still has a rich heritage of nineteenth-century architecture. The main street is named after former premier and state president, John Vorster, who spent

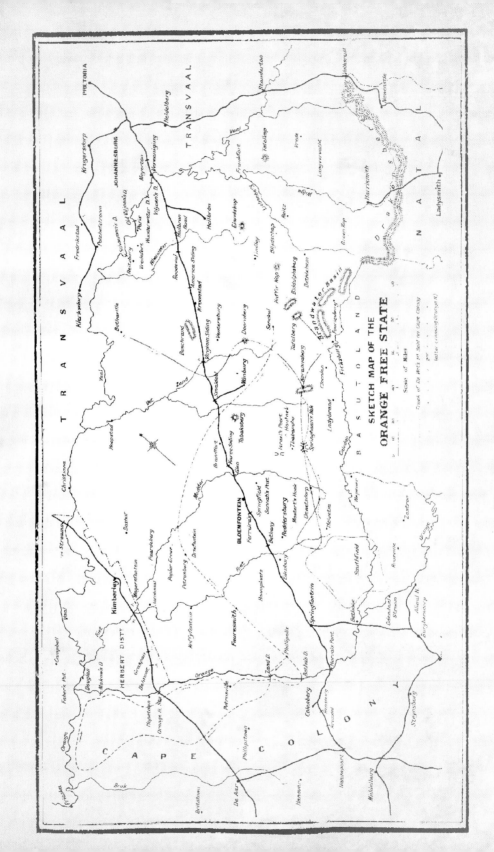

SKETCH MAP OF THE

ORANGE FREE STATE

much of his childhood there. At Sterkstroom, Churchill noticed a line of empty trenches, a hospital flying the Red Cross flag and an extension to the cemetery enclosure where there were fresh graves from the war. Then, passing through Molteno, the train reached Stormberg Junction. A few months earlier, on 9 December 1899, Major General William Gatacre had launched an attack here on the Boers under Commandant Jan Olivier, having gathered his troops for several days. Stormberg lies in a basin, and on the heights above it the Boers were entrenched, not in great numbers but supported by artillery. The attack ended in disaster for the British – some 634 soldiers, including officers, were captured. Now there were few traces left of the Boers' occupation, only the litter of tins, straw and paper, and, as Churchill also notes, the grave of Commandant Hans Swanepoel. (Swanepoel was in fact wounded, not killed, so Churchill got his facts wrong here.)[6]

At Stormberg, Churchill learnt that no immediate advance from Bloemfontein was likely or even possible for a fortnight, and therefore decided to proceed to Cape Town, having had to cover a distance of 700 miles in two days. Because of the war, some sections of the railway had only just reopened. At Stormberg, Churchill diverted west to Rosmead Junction. Originally known as Middelburg Road, this was a Cape Government Railway station, established in 1883, when the railway line from Cradock was inaugurated. The little village now lay at the junction of the Western, Midland and Eastern Railway systems, and was therefore important to the military and economic affairs of the region. In 1898, two years before Churchill stopped there, it had been renamed Rosmead in honour of Sir Hercules Robinson, governor of the Cape, who was appointed Lord Rosmead in 1896. The village had been occupied by Boer forces in October 1899, but after the Battle of Modder River on 28 November 1899, they retreated and abandoned the field to the British.

The next stop was Naauwpoort, a station that was built on part of the Hartebeeshoek Farm with the diversion of the railway line to Colesberg in 1883–84. Situated on barren veld dotted with stone koppies, it was named Naauwpoort after the adjacent farm, and in 1963 the name was changed to Noupoort. Private J.W. Milne of the Gordon Highlanders wrote of Naauwpoort at the time:

British lookout post at Rosmead Junction during the war

The railway village of Rosmead today

The British camp at Naauwpoort

There is nothing but big hills all round about and a few houses about the
Station. There were plenty of troops here. A lot of them were the sick
and the wounded. There is a big base Hospital here I was told. There are
about 800 in it. There are about 20 Boer P.O.W. here, big strong men by
us. They are kept in a place fenced with corrugated iron and a barbed
wire on the top, guarded by soldiers day and night.[7]

Years ago Naauwpoort was a busy junction, with almost 100 trains passing
through every day. The old All Saints Anglican Church in town was built
by stonemasons from the British ranks garrisoned there during the war.
Another remnant from the war is the circular whitewashed blockhouse,
which seems not to have been built for that purpose, but was converted from
an old windmill. In the local cemetery there is also a garden of remembrance
commemorating the soldiers killed during the war.

From Naauwpoort, the train continued through to De Aar, then a large
military supply depot lying in a typically harsh Karoo landscape. Subdivided
into plots of land in 1839, the town was named after the strong perennial spring

Olive Schreiner in the year
before the outbreak of war

The British camp at De Aar

there and was established as a major junction on the line between Cape Town and Kimberley in 1881. Originally the station was called Brounger Junction, after the head of the railways, William Brounger, but the name never stuck. In time it was to become the second major junction in South Africa after Germiston in the Transvaal. The well-known author Olive Schreiner came to live in De Aar five years after the war until 1913, when her husband, Samuel Cronwright-Schreiner, was town clerk and market master. The town was dominated by windmills, and Cronwright-Schreiner aptly called it 'a town of windmills; I suppose no town of its size, in South Africa, at any rate, has so many windmills.'[8]

In Lionel James's words, De Aar was

at its best ... a miserable place. Not made – only thrown at the hillside, and allowed by negligence and indifference to slip into the nearest hollow. Too far from the truncated kopjes to reap any benefit from them. Close enough to feel the radiation of a sledge-hammer sun from their bevelled summits – close enough to be the channel, in summer, of every scorching blast diverted by them; in winter, every icy draught. Pestilential place, goal of whirlwinds and dust-devils, ankle-deep in desert drift – prototype of Berber in a sandstorm – as comfortless by night as day.[9]

For a second time, Churchill crossed the Great Karoo between De Aar and Cape Town, a journey that has already been described in Chapter 2. Back in Cape Town he stayed at the Mount Nelson once again, where he found it difficult to find a room, and he does not seem to have enjoyed his stay – he complained about the overcrowding, cold dinners, lack of waiters, and scandal and rumour.

During Churchill's stay at the hotel, British poet and writer Rudyard Kipling and his family were also residing there, but Churchill makes no mention of the great literary figure. The Kiplings had arrived from England on 5 February, and although Kipling had obtained a pass from Lord Roberts to go wherever he pleased, he spent the first few weeks visiting military hospitals in Cape Town. He travelled to the Modder River railhead in an ambulance train and then, after the Battle of Paardeberg, returned with a trainload of wounded. At the invitation of Lord Roberts, he

Rudyard Kipling (seated, centre) with Boer War correspondents he worked with in Bloemfontein

joined *The Friend* newspaper in Bloemfontein on 21 March, witnessed the Battle of Karee Siding on 29 March and returned to Cape Town on 3 April, around the time of Churchill's arrival in the city from the Natal front. The Kiplings departed for London on board the *Tantallon Castle* on 11 April, and were to make several trips back to Cape Town in the following years, the last being in January 1908.

Meanwhile, after their victories, the first reaction of the British government was to let bygones be bygones, an approach Churchill fully supported. On 24 March, while still in Ladysmith, he had telegraphed a report to the *Morning Post* in which he advocated a policy of forgiveness towards the Boers, saying that there was no necessity for punishing rebels who had surrendered. The Boers were only traitors in a legal sense, he argued, and that they had only been obeying their natural instinct to join their own kin; their conduct had been morally less reprehensible than that of the renegade British-born burgher. The message was not well received in Britain, and the *Morning Post* disagreed with his sentiments. On the Natal front, local newspapers condemned him clamorously, but at least in Cape Town he found a sympathetic ear in the High Commissioner, Sir Alfred Milner.

After several days in Cape Town, no pass had reached Churchill to allow him to proceed to Bloemfontein. Fortunately, though, he had two good and well-connected friends at Lord Roberts's headquarters in Ian Hamilton, Roberts's former aide-de-camp, and General Nicholson, who both had free access to Roberts. They informed him that the commander-in-chief, Lord Kitchener, had been offended by some passages in Churchill's account of the reconquest of the Sudan, *The River War*, and that Lord Roberts felt that his chief of staff might resent it if Churchill was attached as correspondent to the main section of the British Army. In addition, a letter to the *Morning Post* written from Natal, in which Churchill had criticised the inadequacy of a sermon preached to the troops on the eve of battle by a Church of England army chaplain, had upset Roberts himself.

In the end, however, Churchill's pass was granted on 11 April and he was free to proceed to Bloemfontein – with the proviso, however, that before taking up duties as war correspondent he should receive an admonition from the military secretary to the commander-in-chief against reckless criticism. Roberts made it clear that it was only 'for your father's sake'.[10]

Churchill took the train from Cape Town to Bloemfontein, traversing the Great Karoo for the third time within a few months. They crossed into the Free State at Norval's Pont, 'a small place with only a few houses round about the Station,' according to Private Milne.[11] Churchill saw the first signs of the great impending British troop movements in the Free State. On the same day that Churchill had started off on his journey, Lord Kitchener had ordered that henceforth all troops must march beyond Springfontein in order to clear the railway lines for the passage of war supplies. So at the time, large British columns were marching along the railway on their way to the front.

The one passenger train in the day stopped at Bethanie, where the British Third Division was camped, and, not wishing to arrive in Bloemfontein at

Sunset over the Orange River at Norval's Pont

The hotel at Norval's Pont. The original structure dates back to well before the Boer War

midnight, Churchill decided to spend the night there and proceed at dawn. At Bethanie, 'there was a big camp, a lot of horses, mules, oxen and transport wagons,' in Private Milne's words.[12] Situated near the Riet River and set in characteristic southern Free State grass veld in the district of Edenburg, Bethanie was founded by the Berlin Missionaries in 1834 for the Korana people. A church was completed in 1845 and extended in 1867. A school was built in 1860, the oldest in the Free State still in use. Under the Group Areas Act, the Tswanas of the mission were moved to Thaba Nchu in 1965, and the buildings became neglected, but fortunately in 2000 the church and school were restored and are in use once again.

At Bethanie, Churchill spoke with the commander of the Third Division, General William Forbes Gatacre, whom he knew from his days in the Sudan. From his corrugated-iron cottage near the station, Gatacre received him kindly, talking about past events and the future. Gatacre, who commanded the British force at Stormberg, had his whole division at last, and action was imminent. But the next morning, he was dismissed from his command and ordered back to England, leaving him a broken and downhearted man.

Churchill found Bloemfontein to be a busy, well-established town. Its prosperity had coincided with the discovery of the Kimberley diamond fields in the 1860s, and it became a major service centre for the diamond industry, and for a while also the inland headquarters for some major financial and commercial concerns. As churches and schools were built, the town grew; it attracted many groups, including Germans, Dutch, Jews, Afrikaners, and black and coloured people. It became a key transit point for those bound for either Kimberley or the Witwatersrand, and the Cape Town–Johannesburg railway link reached Bloemfontein in 1890, nine years before the outbreak of the war.

Eight years before Churchill's visit to Bloemfontein, J.R.R. Tolkien, author of *The Hobbit* and *The Lord of the Rings*, was born in the city on 3 January 1892, though his family left South Africa following the death of his father, Arthur Tolkien, in 1895. Tolkien recorded that his earliest memories were of 'a hot, parched country with a blazing sun, drawn curtains, and a drooping eucalyptus'.[13]

During the occupation, the town had been alive with troops from all the

The Berlin Mission church at Bethanie, *circa* 1870; on the left is the old school building (built in 1860)

colonies of the British Empire, and local businesses did good trade. It was estimated that some 1 400 officers and 32 500 troopers, including 11 500 cavalrymen, had descended on Bloemfontein.

In the Free State capital, Churchill was welcomed cordially by Hamilton and Nicholson, but Lord Roberts remained aloof towards the young correspondent and showed no signs of recognising him. Churchill came upon Roberts one morning in the marketplace, but Roberts acknowledged his salute as if he had been a stranger.

Churchill, however, was not put off by his coldness. An exciting time awaited him. Supplied with good horses and other means of transport by the *Morning Post*, he could move swiftly across the wide Free State plains from one British column to another in anticipation of fighting. And in between the clashes he continually sent telegrams and letters to his newspaper.

11

Towards the Transvaal

*'The wonderful air and climate of South Africa, the magnificent scale
of its landscape, the life of unceasing movement and of continuous
incident made an impression on my mind which even after a quarter
of a century recurs with a sense of freshness and invigoration.
Every day we saw new country... all day long I scampered about
the moving cavalry screens searching in the carelessness of
youth for every scrap of adventure, experience or copy.'[1]*

AFTER THE RELIEF OF LADYSMITH and their defeat in the Free
State, thousands of Boers returned to their homes and took an oath
of neutrality. Nevertheless, Lord Roberts's advance to Pretoria was not
unhindered. At Paardeberg, hundreds of
horses and cattle died and rotted in the
Modder River, and many British soldiers
who had used the river's water contracted
typhoid. At one stage, there were some
4500 men suffering from the disease in
Bloemfontein. Set back by this and the
need to gather supplies, and repair destroyed railway lines and bridges, Roberts
was unable to resume his advance until
3 May 1900. The engineers had to repair
the partially destroyed bridges at Norval's
Pont and Bethulie, and various other
smaller bridges and culverts, and communication by rail had to be established

Yet another British soldier is buried in Bloemfontein as a
result of the devastating typhoid epidemic

Lord Roberts's troops crossing the Modder River

between the army in the Free State and the sea bases at East London, Port Elizabeth and Cape Town.

In the meantime, the Boers embarked on a guerrilla campaign (referred to as 'partisan warfare' by Churchill), which would continue until the signing of the peace treaty on 31 May 1902. By the time Roberts advanced from Bloemfontein, the Boers had had skirmishes and battles with the British at Karee Station (29 March), Sanna's Post (31 March), Mostertshoek near Reddersburg (3–4 April), and Boshof (5 April). They had besieged the British garrison at Jammerbergsdrif near Wepener (9–25 April), skirmished at Wakkerstroom near Dewetsdorp (20 April), Swartkoppiesfontein near Boshof (22 April), and at Israelspoort, Swartlapberg and Tobaberg (Thaba Nchu – end of April). On 3 May they also had an engagement at Brandfort.

Five British brigades were available for the operations in the south-eastern Free State: General Hart's brigade of General Hunter's division at Bethulie; the 3rd and 8th divisions under General Herbert Charles Chermside (who

Free State burghers of the Winburg commando

succeeded Gatacre); General Rundle at Springfontein and Bethanie; 1400 yeomanry and mounted infantry under General John Palmer Brabazon; and General Edward Yewd Brabant's Colonial Brigade of about 2500 men.

Before the advance, Churchill had decided to join the cavalry brigade of General Brabazon, operating in the region south-east of Bloemfontein. He loaded his horses and wagon onto a train, and, on 17 April, went by rail south to Edenburg; he left from there in heavy rains and rested for the night at Reddersburg. Edenburg, nestled in the golden prairies some fifty miles from Bloemfontein, is sheep and cattle country. Founded in 1862 on Rietfontein Farm, it was proclaimed a town the following year. Reddersburg, thirty-five miles south of Bloemfontein, was laid out on Vlakfontein Farm in 1861 and named Reddersburg (Saviour's Fort). This was the site of one of the last victories for the Boers over the British, when General Christiaan de Wet attacked a convoy of 600 of the Royal Irish Rifles on 4 April 1900, at Mostert-shoek, and forced their surrender the next day.

The cavalry had a very pleasant ride from Reddersburg, and it was evening when they came to the camp of the main British column. This was at the foot of a prominent knoll rising from a broad plain, but there were scarcely any tents to be seen, and all over the undulating ground horses and oxen were grazing. The soldiers' suppers were being cooked and the camp was covered with a canopy of white smoke from the hundreds of fires. Churchill finally caught up with the British column on 19 April, eleven miles from Dewetsdorp,[2] at the time occupied by a British garrison. The column was the 8th Division, commanded by Sir Leslie Rundle (later nicknamed 'Sir Leisurely Trundle'), whom Churchill had known from his stint in the Sudan.

The legendary General Christiaan de Wet, the man the British could never catch

Churchill was received courteously by General Rundle, who explained that the whole force would march at dawn. Brabazon's brigade was scouting ahead and early the next morning Churchill rode on to join them, much to Brabazon's delight. Approaching the hills around Dewetsdorp later, they encountered Boers in some strength, but Brabazon's yeomanry occupied the nearest hills. In the evening, General Rundle arrived with his two brigades, while a third brigade under General Barr-Campbell was already on the march from the railway. Brabazon's cavalry meanwhile reconnoitred to test the left of the Boers' position, and this led to one of Churchill's most exciting adventures during the war.

The brigade, including the mounted infantry, about a thousand strong, moved south behind the outpost line, and soon came on the enemy's left flank. The ground fell steeply towards a flat basin with a prominent hill rising from it, behind which lay Dewetsdorp, but out of sight of the troops. Round the hill were about 200 Boers, some mounted and some on foot. They were taken by

Dewetsdorp in 1900

Churchill's saviour:
Trooper Clement Roberts

surprise and made an attempt to outflank the outflanking cavalry, and, just as the British long-range rifle fire forced them to take cover behind the hill, a new group of Boers of about the same number charged into the open, crossing the British front at about 2 000 yards, heading towards a stone koppie on the cavalry's right.

Angus McNeill, commander of Montmorency's Scouts since the latter's death, led a group of some forty to fifty scouts in a charge to try to head them off, with Churchill in tow. The Boers were nearer to the stone koppie than the scouts, but still had the hill to climb. The scouts arrived at a wire fence about a hundred yards from the crest of the koppie, dismounted and, having cut the wire, were about to seize the koppie when a number of Boers appeared. McNeill ordered a retreat, and with bullets flying, Churchill tried to jump on his horse, but it broke away and galloped off wildly. Most of the scouts were already 200 yards off, so Churchill found himself alone, without a horse, and about a mile from the nearest cover. He turned and ran for his life, but suddenly a scout came riding up from his left, and Churchill shouted to him to pick him up. The man stopped at once and Churchill quickly jumped into the saddle behind him. Although the horse was wounded, they managed to scramble to safety.

Describing the incident in the *Morning Post*, Churchill suggested that the scout, Trooper Clement Roberts, deserved the Victoria Cross. But either because Churchill was in Roberts's and Kitchener's bad books, or perhaps merely because the authorities did not regard the trooper's conduct as being worthy of such recognition, not even a minor medal was awarded him. Only seven years later, when Churchill was in a position to authorise a decoration as secretary of state for the colonies, did Trooper Roberts receive the Distinguished Conduct Medal for saving his skin.

Churchill's melodramatics come to the fore again when he meditates on the prospect of his death in battle. Writing from the British camp near Dewetsdorp on 22 April, he wonders whether he will ever again see the white cliffs of Dover, adding that hazards are swooping on him out of the sky and thanking God that he has hitherto come through them unscathed. But he wonders why he is often thrust to the brink and then withdrawn.[3]

Lord Roberts sent another infantry division from Bloemfontein and the whole of General French's three brigades of cavalry in a wide sweeping movement against the Boers around Dewetsdorp from the north-west. In two days this combination was completed, and the Boers retreated north, making their way to Thaba Nchu. On 25 April, the column moved towards Thaba Nchu, across great plains of brown grassland broken here and there by scrub-covered hills. Beyond the Modder River, the ground became gradually more rocky and hilly up to Thaba Nchu mountain, and from there the country rose in a succession of ridges to the high peaks of Basutoland.

Churchill described Thaba Nchu as a small village by English standards, but of comparative commercial importance to the Orange Free State and of undoubted strategic value during that phase of the operations. It stands at the foot of the mountain that bears its name, and is approached from Bloemfontein by a long, broad, flat-bottomed valley, its walls rising gradually higher

Eastern Free State farmland, with the mountains of Lesotho in the background

towards the east. The eastern end is closed by a chain of rocky koppies known as Israelspoort, which form a strong rampart.

Captain Stratford St Leger of the mounted infantry, serving with General French's 1st Cavalry Brigade, recorded a good description of Thaba Nchu village. Travelling through the area in mid-March 1900, he wrote:

> Overshadowing the small straggling village is Thabanchu Mountain, which, with its projecting corner-piece, is a conspicuous landmark for miles round. Thabanchu Mountain, I am told, means the Black Mountain, but the most striking portion of it is the huge block of white granite standing out like a sentinel at its eastern extremity ... Thabanchu, from its associations, is a village of more than passing interest. It nestles on the edge of a small plateau with mountains rising abruptly on the north and the impressive Thabanchu Mountain towering above it on the east ... The village, for the most part, consists of the native location and the missions chapels ... By far the quaintest sight I remember seeing, however, was in one of the Thabanchu stores, the brilliancy of the interior of which, hung with many bright-coloured blankets, handkerchiefs, and chintzes, was in pleasing but violent contrast to the hideous corrugated-iron exterior. Several Baralong ladies were spending their monthly allowance in dress.[4]

Hamilton marched along the valley of Israelspoort on 25 April with his entire force and, following an engagement with the Boers, occupied Thaba Nchu the same night. The next day, French and his cavalry arrived and took over the command from Hamilton. According to Churchill, although he often marched and skirmished with French's column, the general completely ignored him and showed him no sign of courtesy or goodwill. But afterwards he became a great friend, with whom he worked for many years in both peacetime and war.

Churchill had come northwards from Dewetsdorp with the cavalry brigades, and was eyewitness to the operations around Thaba Nchu on 26 and 27 April. Hamilton received orders from Lord Roberts to march north on Winburg in conformity with the general advance of the army. The Thaba Nchu column started out on 30 April, and subsequently fought their way through at Houtnek Poort and conquered Thoba Mountain. Houtnek Poort

A welcome outspan for British soldiers on the march

consists of two parallel grassy ridges separated by a shallow valley, with Thoba
Mountain to the west of the pass. Hamilton's force reached Jacobsrust on
3 May, and the next day the whole army moved on, with Lord Roberts passing
through Brandfort towards Smaldeel and Hamilton continuing his march
on Winburg. On the afternoon of 6 May, General Hamilton entered Winburg
at the head of his troops, and the Union Jack was hoisted in the marketplace.
Churchill had decided to march with Hamilton's force, where he would feel
welcome and at home: his cousin Charles Spencer-Churchill, the Duke of
Marlborough, known as Sunny, was on Roberts's staff, while his brother, John,
was the new assistant military secretary. Churchill caught up with Hamilton's
troops on the outskirts of Winburg. It was the start of a memorable period
for the young war correspondent.

From Winburg they were to embark on a long march of between 400 and
500 miles, which lasted about six weeks with the halts and on which Churchill
marvelled at the wonderful air and climate of the country, and the magnificent scale of its landscape. Twenty-five years later he would still remember it
all vividly. Each day they saw new country and every evening they bivouacked

by the side of a new stream, living on the flesh of the sheep that they drove with them in flocks, and chickens, which they pounced on at deserted farms. In addition, Churchill's wagon had a raised floor with space underneath where he stored the best tinned foods and drink that London could provide – so they had every comfort. During the day, Churchill would scamper about the cavalry looking for adventure or anything that would make good copy for the *Morning Post*.

Before they started out on their march, the force had two days of rest on 7 and 8 May at Winburg, and on the 9th the whole army marched forward again towards the Sand River. The first day's march was not long and by midday they had reached their halting place, a mile south of the river. The headquarters was set up on a large farm close to the wagon track.

Churchill gave an interesting description of the Boer farmstead and its occupants. The farmhouse was the best example of a Dutch homestead he had seen in the 500 miles they had travelled through the Free State – a large square building with a wide verandah, a pretty flower garden in front, and half a dozen barns and stables around the farmhouse. The spruit was dammed to form a large, pleasant pool, where fat ducks and geese hid to avoid becoming soldiers' meals. Except for the front, the farm was enclosed on all sides by a thick line of fir trees. The house consisted of three bedrooms with old-fashioned feather beds and quaint wooden bedsteads, a formal but spacious parlour with dark, bulky furniture, and curious prints and coloured plates on the walls; there was also a kitchen, pantry and storeroom.

The family consisted of the gentleman, who was about sixty, his wife, a few years younger, three grown-up daughters, the owner's spinster sister, and several children or grandchildren of varying ages. In all there were seven sons or grandsons, two married with farms of their own, but at the time all were on commando with the Boers, including a youngster of fourteen. The thought also crossed Churchill's mind that at that moment some might perhaps even have been looking at the soldiers at the farm from the heights across the river.[5]

On the evening of 10 May, the British forces were spread along the southern bank of the Sand River with the Boers positioned on the other side. The British crossed the river the next day and camped in the valley beyond the Boers' position, and an officer with a flag of truce was sent into Ventersburg to demand the surrender of the town. Hoping to secure some supplies, 'particularly bottled beer, before everything should be requisitioned by the army', Churchill followed a cavalry force into the town. To him it was a miserable little place, and not to be compared with Winburg. There were a few good shops and a small hotel, however, where he did find what he was looking for, but the overall impression of the town was one of dirt and squalor. Later in 1900, the Dutch Reformed church, dating from 1891, and the municipal offices were burnt down by the British forces. Rather surprisingly, in 1991 the highly treasured communion cup, looted from the church by the British soldiers in 1900, was found in a pawn shop in San Francisco. It was eventually returned in February 1992 to the church after a great deal of communication. The Ventersburg Road Railway Station, about eleven miles north-west of the town, was renamed Hennenman in 1927 after a prominent local farmer, P.F. Hennenman of Swartpan Farm.

Lord Roberts was aiming to reach Kroonstad the next day, even though the Boers were entrenching a strong position along the Boschrand, just south of the town. But for all their marching, Lord Roberts had to stay at America Siding that night, six miles from the Boschrand position. General Hamilton marched on again at dawn, but they soon realised that the Boers had retreated without giving battle. Churchill was determined to witness the capture of Kroonstad, so he left the cavalry behind to catch up with the 11th Division, and finally overtook the head of the infantry columns about three miles from the town. Roberts entered Kroonstad at about midday with all his staff. Kroonstad was a lively business hub in those days with a considerable number of traders of all kinds, shop owners and other entrepreneurs. It was a convenient stopover between the Cape and the Transvaal, and between Natal and the western regions; it was also a pivotal road and rail link.

'It has the reputation of being one of the prettiest places in the Republic, but even when allowances are made for the circumstances under which we saw it, it does not seem that its fame is just,' Churchill wrote of Kroonstad. 'The town looked a little larger than Winburg, though not nearly so clean and well-kept, and the whole place was smothered in reddish dust, and dried up by the sun.'[6]

Many years later, at the age of ninety-three, Major William Francis Barr, an Australian who later settled in Vryheid, Natal, was able to point out the site

Lord Roberts entering Kroonstad, 12 May 1900

of the British camp at Kroonstad – by the railway bridge near the station. He and the other soldiers would pass under this bridge on their way into town to bathe. He also recalled that soon after the troops had surrounded and then occupied Kroonstad, they were very short of rations: 'I remember the ladies all offering us tea and cakes, which we gladly accepted, because … all we had had was green mealies!'[7]

In the meantime, the Boers had retreated north along the railway, and the seat of Boer government had withdrawn to Lindley, named after the American Presbyterian missionary, Daniel Lindley. Lord Roberts would now advance towards the Boers' position on the Rhenoster River. Hamilton set out on 16 May, and the infantry bivouacked eighteen miles from Kroonstad, while a large Boer force was now retreating before Rundle's column (the 8th Division) northwards to Lindley. Hamilton therefore hurried on to take possession of the heights to the north of the town. General Broadwood took the Boers at Lindley by surprise on 17 May and, after a brief skirmish, the town surrendered. Broadwood then retired to the commanding hill to the north to bivouac, and General Hamilton with the rest of the troops moved on to Lindley, marching through sparsely populated, uncultivated countryside.

They were now in the region known as Riemland, which today roughly includes Heilbron, Petrus Steyn, Lindley, Arlington and Rosendal. During the

Boer prisoners of war at Kroonstad, May 1900

Typical sandstone cliffs of the eastern Free State

A storm brewing over the eastern Free State

early 1800s, these central grasslands were home to vast herds of antelope, and because their hunting yielded large quantities of leather that was manufactured into thongs, the Voortrekkers named the area Riemland, derived from the word meaning 'thong'. As well as game, the Voortrekkers also ran into the Matebeles ruled by King Mzilikazi, with whom they fought a tough battle at Vegkop, twenty-five kilometres south of the present-day Heilbron, in October 1836.

The cavalry bivouacked along the nearer slopes of the high hill to the north of Lindley. Churchill found it to be a pretty little town of white-walled houses with blue-grey corrugated-iron roofs, tucked away at the bottom of an incline and partly hidden by bluegum trees. He rode into Lindley in the afternoon to buy various supplies that his wagon now lacked. He described the town as follows:

> It is a typical South African town, with a large central market square and four or five broad unpaved streets radiating there-from. There is a small clean-looking hotel, a substantial gaol, a church and a schoolhouse. But the two largest buildings are the general stores. These places are the depots whence the farmers for many miles around draw all their necessaries and comforts.
>
> Owned and kept by Englishmen or Scotchmen, they are built on the most approved style. Each is divided into five or six large well-stocked departments. The variety of their goods is remarkable. You may buy a piano, a kitchen range, a slouch hat, a bottle of hair wash, or a box of sardines over the same counter. The two stores are the rival Whiteley's of the country-side; and the diverse tastes to which they cater prove at once the number of their customers, and the wealth which even the indolent Boer may win easily from his fertile soil.[8]

Looking for potatoes, Churchill was directed to an Englishman who showed him his garden and explained how he had dammed a marshy sluit in the side of the hills to irrigate twenty gardens of potatoes, cabbages ('they were beauties'), tomatoes, onions, a vine of sweet white grapes, a bed of strawberries and lots more. The Englishman had only been living there for eight

Lindley in 1900

The town of Lindley today

years, but there was already a long row of leafy trees about twenty feet high. 'The signs of industry impressed me,' Churchill remarked.[9]

Early in the morning of the 20th, Broadwood's cavalry moved away over the northern ridges to the road to Heilbron. Hamilton watched the movement of the rear guard. They eventually crossed the Rhenoster River between Lindley and Heilbron to clear the march of the main army. The army bivouacked on the north bank of the Rhenoster within two marches of the town of Heilbron, where they were heading. Churchill wrote:

Heilbron lies in a deep valley. About it on every side rolls the grassy upland country of the Free State, one smooth grey-green surge beyond another, like the after-swell of a great gale at sea; and here in the trough of the waves, hidden almost entirely from view, is the town itself, white stone houses amid dark trees, all clustering at the foot of a tall church spire. It is a quiet, sleepy little place, with a few good buildings and pretty rose gardens, half-a-dozen large stores, a hotel, and a branch line of its own.[10]

John Bredfield, an East Anglian, described Heilbron at the time as

a typical dorp, with a few stores, an hotel, a church, and some pretty houses with shady stoeps and peach trees planted in their gardens, a happy village with nothing whatever beyond its boundaries but earth, springboks, guinea-fowl, korhaan, mealies, sheep, cattle, hares and stony kopjes upraising their flat heads from leagues of level ground for no reason at all.[11]

The location of the present town was established in the late 1830s by the Voortrekkers, but the town was only inaugurated in 1872/73. Some sources claim that Heilbron was named after the German city Heilbronn in Baden-Württemberg, but others say that when the town was first established, a

The town of Heilbron at the time of the Boer War

Jasper Theron's shop in Heilbron, as Churchill would have seen it. Legend has it that he snaffled a chicken from a plot adjoining the Caledonian Hotel (now the Commercial Hotel) where he stayed

certain L.J. Erasmus said: 'We expect blessing from the fountain, and therefore the name must be Heilbron.' (Heilbron is Dutch for 'fountain of well-being', a reference to the mountain-fed stream providing the town with water.)

Heilbron was, for a short time, the seat of the Boer government before President Steyn – described by a *Times* correspondent as 'a nomad, without influence and without following … wandering from farm to farm'[12] – and his councillors decided to move east towards Bethlehem and eventually the Brandwater Basin, near Fouriesburg.

General De Wet arrived from Kroonstad with his men but soon had to retreat before Broadwood's brigade, and they were pursued for some time before the British turned back. On the way back to Heilbron, Churchill found a few Boer ambulance wagons with two German doctors and their Red Cross helpers. One of the latter remarked, significantly, that it was not a war any more, as the poor Boers had no chance against the great numbers of British. One man introduced himself as the military chaplain to the Dutch forces; whether this was the well-known Reverend Daniël Kestell, author of *Through Shot and Flame*, is not clear.

The British headquarters was set up at Leeuwpoort, a farm belonging to

The old farmhouse at Leeuwpoort, where the British set up headquarters and where Churchill acquired a bottle of preserved peaches from the family

Johan Frederik Weilbach, outside Heilbron. During a visit there, Churchill was given a bottle of preserved peaches by the Weilbach daughters. Mrs Weilbach's granddaughter recalled that her grandmother could not speak English. But her older daughters, Cathy, Marie and Jetta, had attended the Huguenot Seminary in Wellington and spoke fluent English, to Churchill's amazement. Like so many people in Britain, he was under the assumption that the Boers were uneducated and backward. He had a pleasant conversation with the Weilbach girls and showed a lot of interest in their preserved peaches in the pantry. Churchill eventually left the house with a bottle, but whether he paid for it, no one will ever know.[13]

Churchill stayed at the Caledonian Hotel[14] in Heilbron, which he described as a regular country inn, and where he found various British subjects who had been assisting the Boer ambulances, possibly armed with rifles.[15] This claim, though, has to be taken with a pinch of salt.

Soldiers of the Imperial Light Horse are buried in Heilbron's cemetery, but these burials date from the fighting on 7 February 1902 during the action at Katkop, near Heilbron.

12

Cycling through Johannesburg

*'One thing showed with sufficient distinctness to attract and astonish
all eyes. The whole crest of the Rand ridge was fringed with factory
chimneys. We had marched nearly 500 miles through a country which,
though full of promise, seemed to European eyes desolate and wild,
and now we turned a corner suddenly, and there before us sprang
the evidences of wealth, manufacture, and bustling civilisation.
I might have been looking from a distance at Oldham.'[1]*

O N 24 MAY 1900, GENERAL HAMILTON's force marched west from
Heilbron, reached the railway and joined Lord Roberts's main column.
Hamilton was instructed to move his men across the railway line and march
on the drift of the river near Boschbank, shifting from the right of the main
army to the left. They crossed the central line of the railway at America Siding
and marched to the Vaal River, crossing it on 26 May after General Broadwood
with his cavalry had secured the passage during the previous night. The march
north was a memorable one for Churchill.

After they had crossed the Vaal, the country became flat and grassy, like
the Orange Free State, but as the column advanced northwards the ground
became broken by blue hills rising up on the horizon, and the swells of pasture
became more uneven, with patches of wood and scrub. They were approaching the Rand.

By now the Boers were holding a strong position on the Klipriviersberg
mountains. (Today, the Klipriviersberg Nature Reserve still has Anglo-Boer
War fortifications, as well as relics of Sotho/Tswana dwellings from over
300 years ago, an old Voortrekker farmstead and sites from the gold-rush
days.) On 28 May, Hamilton made a short march while French pushed on to

Idle time in a Boer laager

reconnoitre. Churchill rode with General Broadwood, whose brigade covered the advance of Hamilton's column.

They entered a hilly area, which limited their view, and at nine o'clock reached a regular pass between two steep, rocky ridges. From the summit of one of these ridges, they looked across the landscape. To the north lay the dark line of the Klipriviersberg, stretching to the east as far as they could see; to the west there were more grassy slopes, from which rose the long smooth ridge of the Witwatersrand reef. Smoke from numerous veld fires cast a veil over the scene, but they could still distinctly see the whole crest of the Rand ridge fringed with factory chimneys. Churchill remarked that he might have been looking from a distance at an English industrial mill town.

The Boers were ready to evacuate Johannesburg, but sent a strong force

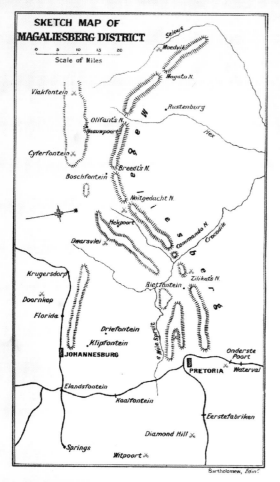

SKETCH MAP OF
MAGALIESBERG DISTRICT

Scale of Miles
0   5   10   15   20

Selous
Moedvik
Magato N.
Vlakfontein
Olifant's N.
Nauwpoort
Cyferfontein
Breedt's N.
Boschfontein
Noitgedacht N.
Hekpoort
Dwarsvlei
Commando N.
Crocodile
Krugersdorp
Zilikat's N.
Rietfontein
Doornkop
Florida
Driefontein
Klipfontein
JOHANNESBURG
Onderste Poort
PRETORIA
Waterval
Elandsfontein
Kaalfontein
Eerstefabriken
Diamond Hill
Springs
Witpoort

Rustenburg
Hex
of Mile Spruit

Bartholomew, Edin.

to oppose the advance of Hamilton's column at Florida, on the Johannesburg–Potchefstroom route. Orders from the British headquarters for 29 May were that French, with the cavalry division, was to march around Johannesburg to Driefontein; Hamilton was to go to Florida; while the main army under Roberts was to occupy Germiston and seize the junctions of the Natal, Cape Colony and Potchefstroom lines. Advancing with great speed through Elandsfontein Station, Lord Roberts surprised the Boers in Germiston, and after a brief skirmish occupied the town. French had camped for the night south of the Klip River, and on the morning of 29 May moved westwards, clearing several of the hills to almost two miles north of the drainage line of the Klip River before he was held back by the enemy. Churchill had a fortunate escape when, riding across the slopes with General Smith-Dorrien, who commanded one of Hamilton's brigades, into lines of smoke from veld fires started by the Boers, he missed the left flank of the Gordon Highlanders on the ridge. Emerging through the smoke curtain, they suddenly found themselves only a few yards from the enemy. When shot at, they charged back into the smoke, escaping unharmed. Churchill's luck had saved him once again.

French halted his brigades and waited for Hamilton. When they continued the fight, all the Boers west of the town under generals De la Rey and Viljoen retreated northwards towards Pretoria. And in conjunction with Roberts's movements, the British brought about the surrender of the whole of the Witwatersrand.

British troops outside Johannesburg before the occupation

British troops entering Johannesburg

Major William Francis Barr recalled the British capture of Johannesburg:

On the 29th we moved in to surround Johannesburg. This was one of the most magnificent sights I have ever seen … we moved in at a steady canter towards Germiston via Rosettenville … it was all open ground – a magnificent sight. Wherever you looked, you could see horses which had fallen into ant-bear holes, with their legs sticking straight up into the air. As we moved along the Boers fired at us … After this action we moved forward, on to Germiston Station then on to Knight's Deep. The trains were pulling out of Jo'burg as fast as they could, and at Knight's Deep the gangers had piled dolomite trucks onto the rails to prevent any more trains from getting out … we pushed on past the headgear of this mine and then galloped on into Germiston Station. There were hundreds of civilians waiting there … that afternoon we pushed on to Malvern, overlooking Cyrildene, and went into camp … No one got out of Jo'burg after that and on this, the 31st May, Jo'burg surrendered.[2]

French continued his march to Driefontein, while Hamilton entered Florida and found there and at Maraisburg sufficient stores until his convoys arrived. Churchill described Florida as the Kew Gardens of Johannesburg, where a well-built dam across the broad valley formed a beautiful lake, surrounded by plantations of Australian pines. Behind these rose the black-and-white pointed chimneys of the mines. There was a small but comfortable hotel, The Retreat, which on Sundays was popular among the weary speculators. Signs of industry and commerce were to be seen everywhere along the reef – flashy advertisements, telegraph and telephones lines, and the ground marked out with obelisks of stone into deeps and concessions, and labelled with all the names of the companies in the market columns of the newspapers.

Churchill was eager to go into Johannesburg to telegraph news of the capitulation of the city. While he was standing on the verandah of the temporary British headquarters, two cyclists arrived from the direction of the town. One of them was a Frenchman, Lautre, who had come from the Langlaagte mine, where he said he had seen no Boers. Lautre agreed to act as guide to

British troops take down the Transvaal flag on 31 May 1900

Churchill in Johannesburg. At the same time, Hamilton took the opportunity to send a more detailed account of his arrival in Florida. Churchill borrowed Lautre's friend's bicycle, and the two set off, Churchill dressed in a plain suit and a soft cap. Lautre had warned him that if stopped by Boers, he should speak French.

The tracks they cycled along were bad, and they wound up and down hills, and frequently through sand, but they managed to make good progress on the bicycles. Lautre knew the area well and, avoiding all the highways, led Churchill from one mine to another, around the heaps of mine tailings, between vast sheds of machinery, across tram lines and through thick copses of fir trees.

At Langlaagte, they found one of Major Rimington's scouts pushing towards the town, who told them that he was uncertain of the situation ahead, except that he knew that British troops had not yet entered Johannesburg. As the two hurried on along their route, downhill for the most part, it became more built up with houses. At around sunset the track turned into a proper road. Avoiding the main thoroughfares, they cycled through the poorer quarters, where 'moody-looking people chatted at the street cor-

Soldiers and civilians cheering after the fall of Johannesburg

ners, and eyed us suspiciously'.³ All the shops were shut and most of the houses had their windows boarded up. Crossing a side street, they saw three mounted Boers, but they rode on unhindered into the central square, where Lautre, speaking in French, pointed out the post office and other public buildings to Churchill. At one stage, a Boer pulled his horse into a walk beside them, but when he heard them speaking French, he turned away and cantered on.

As they approached the south-eastern outskirts of the town, the streets became more deserted, and they found themselves alone. Eventually they encountered three British soldiers from Maxwell's brigade looking for food, and the five men proceeded together. There was no picket line at the edge of the city, but as they walked on they soon found themselves in the middle of a large bivouac of Maxwell's brigade. Churchill met some old acquaintances, from whom he learnt that Lord Roberts's headquarters were at Germiston, about seven miles away. They continued along paths through dense forests of fir, and their route meant they had to scale wire fences and walk through ditches and holes. They reached the railway after about an hour and made their way towards camp fires they could see in the distance, where they came

Johannesburg, *circa* 1900

upon another bivouac and General Tucker's mess. Churchill had known Tucker from his days in India when he was stationed at Secunderabad. Tucker had been sent late in the afternoon to join forces with French to complete the cordon around Johannesburg, but darkness had overtaken them.

After some whisky and water, Churchill and Lautre set off again for Lord Roberts's headquarters two miles beyond Germiston. From a slope they could make out the glittering lights of the 11th Division's camp. After half an hour, they came to a firm road and could cycle again. Twenty minutes later, they were in Germiston and went into the hotel, where Churchill found Lionel James, the principal correspondent of *The Times*. His subordinate had not yet arrived from Hamilton's force. They dined hastily and set off again, reaching the camp two miles further on. At about 10:30 p.m., they reached the building housing the division's headquarters. They sent off their dispatches via an orderly, and after a few minutes Lord Roberts asked to see them. Churchill was struck by Roberts's extraordinary eyes, and in his writings marvelled at the different emotions they could convey – blazing with anger, with hot yellow fire behind them; grey as steel and cold and uncompromising; or twinkling brightly with pleasure.

Churchill told the field marshal all he knew, after which Roberts offered them beds for the night. It was Churchill's first comfortable bed in a month and, dead tired, he soon fell asleep.

Some time later, in early June, his aunt, Lady Sarah Wilson, also came to Johannesburg. She had previously described the town she had found four years earlier as

> light-hearted, reckless, and enterprising ... I fell under the fascination of what was then a wonderful town, especially wonderful from its youth. The ever-moving crowds which thronged the streets, every man of which appeared to be full of important business and in a desperate hurry, reminded one of the City in London. Smart carriages with well-dressed ladies drove rapidly past, the shops were cunningly arranged with tempting wares.[4]

Now, during the war, she was still pleased that the shops were open and wonderfully well supplied – except for butter and cigarettes, which were lacking. She had lunch the next day at a grill room called Frascati's, one of the fashionable restaurants at the time, an underground venue where the cuisine was first rate and the place thronging with civilians of many nationalities. She also went to see some of the major mines, including the Ferreira Deep, which by then had been operated by the Transvaal government for the last eight months.

Lady Sarah Wilson was planning to go on to Pretoria, where by strange coincidence she was to bump into her nephew Winston.

13

The fall of Pretoria

*'We passed through a narrow cleft in the southern wall of mountains,
and Pretoria lay before us – a picturesque little town with red
or blue roofs peeping out among masses of trees, and here
and there an occasional spire or factory chimney.'[1]*

ALTHOUGH ROBERTS HAD WANTED TO push through to Pretoria, his troops' fatigue and having to wait for supplies meant a two-day halt. The advance was resumed on 3 June. The left flank consisted of the cavalry division under French; the centre was formed by Hamilton's force; and the right or main column nearest the railway comprised the 7th and 11th divisions, Colonel James Gordon's cavalry brigade and the corps troops, all under the command of Lord Roberts.

The west side of Pretoria at the turn of the century

The east side of Pretoria

In the meantime, on 29 May, President Paul Kruger had left Pretoria for Machadodorp in the eastern Transvaal, and the seat of the Boer government had been moved to Middelburg, on the Delagoa Bay line. (Kruger was to eventually sail for Holland on 19 October. He died in exile in Clarens, Switzerland.) On 30 and 31 May, the government stores in Pretoria were looted, and General Louis Botha had to step in to try to restore some order. It was against this background that Roberts's force converged on the Transvaal capital. A *Times* correspondent wrote that 'the greatest consternation prevailed in Pretoria. There was no discipline at the front, and it seemed that all cohesion had left the commandos. The town itself was in a state of chaos.'[2]

The British force reached Sesmylspruit on 3 June, the same day their advance had commenced. There the Boers under Lucas Meyer and Jan Smuts were occupying the hills sloping down to the spruit. At dawn on 4 June, Hamilton's column, marching on Elandsfontein, was diverted with orders to bivouac on Pretoria Green, west of the town, while Gordon hurried to the Delagoa Bay railway line to try to cut off the Boers' last avenue of escape.

Lord Roberts thrust his artillery well forward, supported by Hamilton and

Lord Roberts rides through Pretoria

Colonel Henry's mounted troops. The artillery of the 7th Division started firing, and the Boers replied with brisk rifle fire. Fort Schantzkop and Fort Klapperkop, unmanned by the Boers, and the railway station and magazines were heavily bombarded, and the Boers retreated in haste through the town. Churchill later remarked that if the Boers had defended Pretoria with their forts and guns they could have held back the British for several weeks. But before dusk, their whole position was occupied by the infantry. An officer bearing a flag of truce was sent into town to demand the surrender, and the next day, the civil authorities surrendered Pretoria. General Louis Botha ordered all commandos still in and around Pretoria to fall back to Eerste Fabrieken.

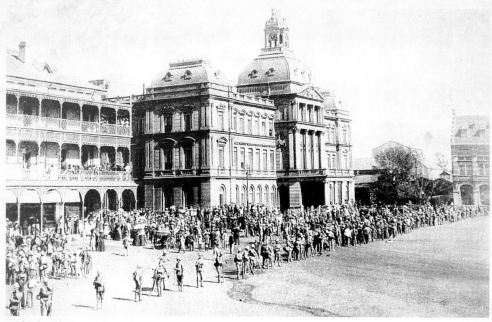
Lord Roberts's troops in Pretoria, 5 June 1900

Hamilton's force swept round the western side into the town, and Churchill hurried along with his cousin, the Duke of Marlborough, soon overtaking General Pole-Carew, who was advancing towards the railway station. They passed through a narrow cleft in the southern wall of mountains, and there lay Pretoria before them – a picturesque town, as Churchill observed.

At the station, a train loaded with Boers still managed to escape, but several other trains remained behind and a company of grenadiers captured the Boers occupying them. After further delay, the guards entered the town along the main street and made their way towards the central square. Anxious to know what had happened to his fellow prisoners from his days spent at the Staatsmodelskool, Churchill and his cousin found a mounted Dutchman who undertook to guide them to where they were imprisoned. After three-quarters of a mile, they crossed a little brook before coming to a long tin building surrounded by dense security wire. Churchill raised his hat and cheered, and immediately the cry was answered from within. The Duke of Marlborough called on the commandant to surrender, and the prisoners

The release of British POWs at the Staatsmodelskool

rushed out of the house into the yard as the sentries threw down their rifles, and the rest of the guards were surrounded by the British officers and their weapons seized. One Grimshaw of the Dublin Fusiliers produced a Union Jack, which he had made during his imprisonment out of a Vierkleur. The Transvaal flag was lowered and, amid wild cheers, the British flag hoisted.

One of the released prisoners was Frederick Maurice Crum, who, in his book *With the Mounted Infantry in South Africa*, provided a lively account of their release:

Tuesday, June 5th. – About 8 a.m. large bodies of men were visible to the west, about seven miles off, but it was impossible to say whether they were our men or Boers. Even if they were our men it was possible that we should be hustled off under their noses. About 9 a.m., two men in felt hats and khaki with a civilian galloped up. Even till they were a

Released British POWs march through Pretoria

hundred yards off I feared they might be Boers. Then they took off their
hats and waved them. There was a yell, and we all rushed through the
gate. They were Marlborough and Winston Churchill, and we were free!
We jolly soon had the Boer flag down, and the soldier servants, armed,
on sentry over the Hollanders inside as prisoners. A Union Jack, made by
one of our fellows for the great moment, was hoisted. Majendie and I
tore down the hill into the town, running and yelling. It was a grand
feeling being free again. When we got into the town we found British
sentries over all the Government buildings, Kruger's house, and all the
banks, &c.[3]

The commandant formally surrendered 129 officers and 39 soldiers, whom
he had in his custody, and also surrendered, besides himself, four corporals
and forty-eight Dutchmen. The latter were confined within the wire cage and

guarded by the released British prisoners, but they were later permitted to take the oath of neutrality and return to their homes.

At two o'clock, Lord Roberts and his staff and the foreign attachés entered the town, and proceeded to the central square, where the town hall, Parliament House, and other public buildings were situated. Here the British flag was hoisted over Parliament House and the army paraded past it, with Pole-Carew's division coming from the south and Ian Hamilton's from the west as the townsfolk looked on.

German volunteer Franco Seiner, who had come all the way from Germany to fight with the Boers, described the Pretoria of 1900 as a place with 20 000 whites and 10 000 blacks, a state library with 14 000 volumes, a museum and ten churches. A fairly primitive horse tram connected the various suburbs. Most houses were set in gardens, lying between bluegums, willow and camphor trees, ivy and other creepers. 'In general we are well off here,' he wrote. 'The beer is light, the wine heavy, the water tastes bad.'[4]

Churchill booked a room in the Grand Hotel in Pretoria with a balcony overlooking Church Square. He had a surprise when on 7 June he bumped into his aunt, Lady Sarah Wilson, who had left Mafeking on 4 June for Pretoria. From here she and a Mrs Godley were to go on to Cape Town, from where they were to sail back to England.

Lady Sarah Wilson had visited Pretoria four years previously, and described her experiences in her memoirs:

As Pretoria was approached the country became very pretty: low hills and many trees, including lovely weeping-willows, appeared on the landscape, and away towards the horizon was situated many a snug little farm; running streams caught the rays of the sun, and really rich herbage supplied the pasture for herds of fat cattle. The town itself did not prove specially interesting. An imposing space called Church Square was pointed out to us with great pride by the Dutch gentleman who kindly did cicerone. There we saw the little primitive 'Dopper' church where the President always worshipped, overshadowed and dwarfed by the magnificent Houses of Parliament, built since the Transvaal acquired riches, and by the no less grand Government Offices.[5]

At Pretoria, she found accommodation at the Grand Hotel, which was at capacity. The polite manager found her a room, which he said would be free in a few hours, as the gentleman occupying it was to depart soon. To her surprise, it turned out to be her nephew, Winston Churchill, who gave up part of his suite for her use. Men in khaki swarmed all over the crowded hotel, and no fewer than a hundred officers were dining that night in the large restaurant.[6]

Early next day, Churchill and the two ladies drove out to see the departure of General Baden-Powell and his staff, who were leaving to rejoin their men at Rustenburg. They were delighted when Lord Roberts, riding alongside Baden-Powell, stopped to speak to them. 'I shall, however, never forget how kindly he spoke nor the inexpressible sadness of his face,' Lady Sarah recalled. 'I told him how quiet everything appeared to be along the road we had taken, and how civil were all the Boers we had met.' They spent the rest of the day and the next on a tour of the town, and Lady Sarah remarked that 'it certainly presented far more to interest a visitor than on the occasion of my last visit in 1896'. General French and his staff had established themselves at the Netherlands Club, while Lord Roberts had set up his headquarters at the Residency in Sunnyside. Close by there was a charming villa for General Brabazon, Lord Dudley, John Ward and Captain W. Bagot. 'The surroundings of these dwellings were exceedingly pretty, with shady trees, many streams, and a background of high hills crowned by forts, which latter were just visible to the naked eye,'[7] she recalled. From Sunnyside they went to look at Fort Schantzkop and Fort Klapperkop (called 'Kapper Kop Fort' by Lady Sarah). The view from Klapperkop was magnificent. Conducted by Churchill, they finally inspected the 'Bird-cage', where the British officers had been imprisoned, and the Staatmodelskool, from where Churchill had made his escape.

But despite the positive impressions, Pretoria at the time was not a normal town. 'After a day in Pretoria we realized that, in spite of the shops being open and the hotels doing a roaring trade, notwithstanding the marvellous organization visible on all sides, events were not altogether satisfactory,' Lady Sarah wrote, 'and one noted that the faces of those behind the scenes were grave and serious.'[8]

The mild resistance the Boers had put up in the face of the British advance from Bloemfontein, and the fall of Pretoria, raised British hopes that they would ask for peace, but the successes gained in the Free State by General De Wet encouraged the Boers under General Louis Botha in the Transvaal. On 8 June, an armistice was observed by both sides, and Lord Roberts was to meet the republican generals at Zwartkop on the 9th. But when the 9th came, Botha declined, which resulted in the resumption of operations.

The military situation was that Lord Roberts's army was spread in and around Pretoria mostly on the eastern and north-eastern sides of the town, while the Boers under Botha and De la Rey held a strong position some fifteen miles to the east on the Delagoa Bay Railway. It was therefore Roberts's intention to drive the 6 000 armed Boers from the district and a series of combined operations was begun. He left the 14th Brigade to hold Johannesburg and the 18th Brigade to garrison Pretoria, leaving only the 11th Division, the corps troops and Hamilton's force free for field operations.

The Boers' position ran along a high line of steep hills that extended north and south for some twenty-five miles from Doornfontein, north of Pretoria, to Kleinzonderhout, south-east of Pretoria. Roberts's strategy was to turn both flanks with cavalry forces and cut the line behind the Boers. So on 11 and 12 June he tried to break through the Boer positions along the line of the Diamond Hill plateau (also known as Donkerhoek, after the farm), but it was not until nightfall of 11 June that he was able to make any progress. The Boers put up strong resistance, but in the end the superior numbers of the British began to tell. On the night of 12/13 June, the Boers abandoned their positions and moved eastwards.

Although Churchill gives a full account of the Battle of Diamond Hill, he only mentions in passing his own involvement in the action. General Hamilton, however, speaks of Churchill's 'conspicuous gallantry' when he single-handedly went scouting up the hill until he found a protected niche high up, from where he waved a handkerchief on a stick to indicate the way up.[9] Hamilton believed Churchill came so close to the Boers that he could easily have been shot. From General Ben Viljoen's account of the battle, however, General Tobias Smuts was by then already abandoning the Boers' position at the summit. Nevertheless, Churchill would not have been aware of this, so his feat was no less daring.

Following the action on Diamond Hill, the whole army returned to Pretoria, leaving only a mounted infantry corps to hold the conquered positions. French and Pole-Carew were given a much-needed rest, while Hamilton was soon sent off on his travels again. Lord Roberts had taken possession of Bloemfontein, the Rand and Pretoria, and the greater part of the railways was in British hands. Nevertheless, the Boers were not yet conquered and would drag the war out for almost another two years.

For Churchill, though, the war had come to an end, but it was with mixed feelings that he watched the departure of the column with which he had spent such a long time and seen so much action. Lord Roberts came himself to see them off. The two cavalry brigades marched past, then Ridley's mounted infantry, then General Bruce Hamilton's infantry brigade with the City Imperial Volunteers, and lastly miles of transport wagons and men, leaving a trail of red Transvaal dust until they finally vanished through the gap in the southern hills.

With the operations at an end, Churchill had decided to return home. The war had become a guerrilla campaign and looked to become shapeless and indefinite. He also had an eye on the general elections back home. So with the consent of the authorities, he resumed full civilian status and boarded the train for Cape Town. The train had many carriages and was crowded with soldiers from several regiments who were being sent south or home. Little did Churchill know that there would be one last adventure in store for him.

When they were beyond Koppies Station, about 100 miles south of Johannesburg, in the early morning – Churchill was having breakfast – the train jerked to a halt. Churchill and the soldiers climbed down on to the line, and the next moment a shell from a small Boer gun burst near them. About a hundred yards ahead, a temporary wooden bridge was in flames. The soldiers began to get out of the carriages, but no one was in command. Memories of the armoured-train ambush of 15 November the previous year came back. With the fortified camp at Koppies Station in mind, Churchill ran along the railway line to the engine and ordered the engine driver to

Going home! British troops wait to board a Cape Town-bound train

blow his whistle to make the soldiers board the train again, and to steam back to Koppies Station.

Less than a hundred yards away in the dry watercourse under the burning bridge they saw a number of Boers – the last Churchill was to encounter in wartime. He fitted the wooden stock to his Mauser pistol and fired six or seven shots at them, and the Boers scattered without firing back. The engine then steamed off and they were soon safely at Koppies Station. At Koppies they heard that a fierce action was in progress at Heuningspruit (called 'Honing Spruit' by Churchill), a station further down the line, and that the train before theirs had been held up. The men at Heuningspruit nevertheless succeeded in holding out till the next day when reinforcements arrived, and the Boers retreated. Anticipating that it was going to take several days to repair the railway line, the soldiers borrowed horses and marched all night without incident from Koppies Station to Kroonstad with a troop of Australian lancers.

A Boer commando

Back in Cape Town, Churchill was reunited with his valet, Thomas Walden, and they sailed for England on the *Dunnottar Castle*, the same ship that had brought them to South Africa nine months earlier. During the voyage, he occupied himself with completing another book, *Ian Hamilton's March*. They reached Southampton on 20 July 1900, to yet another enthusiastic welcome from the crowd.

In South Africa, many people expected the war to be over soon. *The Times* reported rather optimistically:

Despite the fact that the greater portion of the British Army in the Transvaal and Orange River Colony had been for the past two months or

Boer women and children were rounded up and taken to concentration camps

more engaged in the uncongenial task of 'sitting tight', much has been accomplished which in the immediate future may be expected to produce important results. Organization has prepared the way for the final swoop which will surely finish the war, and the end, which, to the superficial observer, possibly seems an indefinite distance away, is really so close at hand that those well-informed people scout the idea that the struggle will continue for a longer period than another three months at the most.[10]

The Norval's Pont concentration camp memorial

Under the British scorched-earth policy, which involved burning down the Boers' farmsteads, slaughtering their livestock and the notorious concentration camps for Boers, including women and children, the land was devastated. Boer commandos continued to operate in the Transvaal and Orange Free State,

A plaque commemorating those who died in the Norval's Pont concentration camp

and a few under General Jan Smuts in the Cape Colony. But on 31 May 1902, when most of the commandos were on their last legs, the peace treaty was signed at Vereeniging. For many of these men, there was nothing to go home to: their farms had been burnt to the ground, their wives and children lost through disease in the concentration camps, and they had no money. After the treaty there followed many years of rebuilding the former Boer republics, but the bitterness remained for a long time to come.

Conclusion

O N RETURNING HOME TO ENGLAND, Churchill received a memorable welcome in the constituency of Oldham, which he was to contest in the coming elections. He entered the town in a state procession of ten landaus, and drove through streets crowded with enthusiastic supporters. He described his escape to a gathering in the Theatre Royal, and discovered that the wife of Mr Dewsnap, the Oldham engineer who had lowered Churchill down the Witbank mine, was in the audience. In the 1900 general elections, he was elected to the House of Commons by a narrow margin of 230 votes. He would spend more than sixty years in Parliament.

After the war, he undertook a lecture tour in the United States and published *London to Ladysmith via Pretoria* and *Ian Hamilton's March*.

The American writer Mark Twain

Throughout his tour of the US, he received the help of eminent Americans, such as senators Bourke Cockran and Chauncey Depew, and other leading politicians, and his opening lecture in New York was under the auspices of the famous author Mark Twain (real name, Samuel Langhorne Clemens). By then Twain was old and grey, but had a most delightful conversational style, according to Churchill. They argued about the war, and Churchill had no answer to Twain's statement that when a poor country is fighting for its life, war could probably be justified, but that was not the case with Britain.

By the middle of February 1901, when the tour had come to an end, Churchill was exhausted. For more than five months, almost

A pro-Boer French publication

every night, except for Sundays, and often twice a day, he had spoken for an hour or more, and had been constantly travelling. His reward, however, was substantial – he received nearly £10 000, which made him financially independent for the future, and allowed him to concentrate on a career in politics.

In 1906, after a disagreement over Neville Chamberlain's tariff-reform policy, Churchill crossed the floor to join the Liberal Party. He married Clementine Hozier in September 1908, with whom he enjoyed a long and happy marriage. They had a son and three daughters. He became president of the Board of Trade under Asquith's Liberal cabinet and later, as home secretary in 1910–11, worked for special reform with David Lloyd George. As first lord of the Admiralty in 1911, he did much to modernise the navy. His role in World War I was controversial, especially after the Gallipoli campaign, and he resigned from the Admiralty. He then served as a battalion commander in France, and joined Lloyd George's coalition government. Between 1917 and 1922, he filled several top positions, including secretary for war and minister of munitions. With the collapse of the Liberal Party in 1922, he found himself out of Parliament for two years, but returned in 1924 as Chancellor of the Exchequer under Baldwin's Conservative government.

He was denied office between 1929 and 1939 because of disagreements with the ruling party on India, rearmament and Chamberlain's appeasement policy, but in September 1939 he was reinstated to the Admiralty. The following year, he succeeded Chamberlain as prime minister and led Britain through the Second World War. His conferences with Roosevelt and Stalin did much to shape post-war Europe. He was defeated in the general elections in July 1945, and became leader of the opposition before becoming prime minister again after the 1951 elections.

On 1 April 1953, he received a knighthood of the Most Noble Order of the Garter, thereby becoming Sir Winston Churchill. In the same year he received the Nobel Prize in Literature. He resigned as premier in 1955, mainly due to his age and poor health, and dedicated his last years to writing and painting. He died on 25 January 1965 at the age of ninety, and was buried in Oxfordshire next to his parents and brother, John, at Bladon churchyard, near Blenheim Palace.

Churchill's association with the mining officials at Witbank, who helped him escape in December 1899, had an interesting sequel. On 25 February 1901, Churchill wrote a letter from England to John Howard, the Witbank mining manager who had facilitated his escape. In the letter, Churchill said that he would send eight gold watches to South Africa to thank the mine personnel who had helped him escape from Witbank to Lourenço Marques. The watches were to be sent to the Standard Bank in Cape Town the following week, and he asked Howard and one of his officials to fetch the package from the bank. In the letter, Churchill wrote the names of the eight men who had helped him, and on the back of the nineteen-carat watches would be engraved the inscription 'From Winston S. Churchill in recognition of timely help afforded him in his escape from Pretoria during the South African War. Dec. 13 1899.'

John Adams, the mine secretary, went to Cape Town on holiday and fetched the parcel at the bank. It was opened in Witbank later, but to their shock, there were only seven watches, and not one for Howard. His name was not even on the list that Churchill had given to his secretary. They notified Churchill of this oversight, but Howard never received a thing.

Enemies in 1900, Allies forty years later. General Jan Smuts and Churchill with Mrs Churchill during World War II

The story behind the watches was carefully researched by Jimmy McLachlan, a former colonel from World War II. Jimmy and his brother Archie opened the Boulevard Hotel in 1954 in Pretoria, and in 1968 decided to open another in Witbank. He was looking for some link with Witbank's history for a name for the hotel, and when he saw the letter that Churchill had written to Howard displayed in the Staatsmodelskool, decided there and then to name the bar in the hotel after Churchill.

McLachlan wrote a letter to Churchill's widow, Lady Clementine Spencer, asking permission, and in a letter dated 3 October 1966 she consented. McLachlan even visited Scotland to do research on the watches. Howard's son Lewis wrote from Germany that his father had suspected that Churchill had sent his watch separately. In his research, McLachlan determined the names of seven people who had to receive the watches. They were John Howard (mine manager), Daniel Dewsnap (mine engineer), Joe McKenna (mine captain), Charles Burnham (storeman and dealer), Dr James Gillespie (mine doctor), John McHenry (miner) and John Adams (mine secretary).

According to McLachlan, Howard probably fled when the Boers had found out who had helped Churchill escape. The field cornet, however, was a friend of his and gave Howard time to disappear before he could be caught.

McLachlan had seen the watch sent to Dewsnap, then in the possession of his grandson. McKenna's watch was inherited by his daughter and she left Zimbabwe for England with it. Burnham's watch was found in the Killie Campbell Museum in Durban, while Gillespie's watch had gone to Scotland. It is suspected that McHenry had his watch on him when he was shot down during World War I, and Adams's watch was destroyed in a fire.

Celia Sandys, Churchill's granddaughter, told McLachlan that she thinks Churchill also sent two watches to two women, the domestic servant and cook at the mine hostel. She gave him the names of nine people she believes Churchill wanted to send the watches to: Howard, Adams, Gillespie, Dewsnap, McKenna, McHenry, Burnham, Ada Blunden (the domestic servant) and Ellen David (the cook). In a note to his secretary, however, Churchill only provided eight names. Whether the two ladies received their watches is not known.

There is still a photograph of Daniel Dewsnap with the watch given to him by Churchill in Churchill's Bar in the Protea Hotel, Witbank.

Notes

Introduction

1 Sir Frederick Maurice, 'Mr Churchill as a military historian', *Foreign Affairs*, July 1927.

2 Virginia Cowles, *Winston Churchill: The Era and the Man* (New York: Grosset & Dunlap, 1953), p. 66.

3 Hugh Martin, *Battle: The Life Story of Winston Churchill* (London: Victor Gallancz, 1940), p. 18.

4 Richard Hough, *Winston & Clementine: The Triumph of the Churchills* (London: Bantam, 1990), p. 129.

5 Martin Gilbert, *Churchill: A Photographic Portrait* (London: Heinemann, 1974), p. 15.

6 Ibid., pp. 27–28.

7 J.B. Atkins, *Incidents and Reflections* (London: Christopher's, 1947), p. 122.

8 Sir Winston Churchill, *My Early Life* (London: Thornton Butterworth, 1930), p. 342.

Chapter 1: Early life and military career

1 Churchill, *My Early Life*, p. 229.

2 Martin Gilbert, *Churchill: A Life* (London: Pimlico, 2000), p. 54.

3 Consuelo, an Alabama belle and budding suffragist (1853–1933), was the only daughter of William Kissam Vanderbilt, a New York railroad millionaire.

4 R. Knox, 'Poor little rich girl', *Tribune Magazine*, 15 May 1953.

5 Aylmer Haldane, *A Soldier's Saga* (Edinburgh and London: William Blackwood & Sons, 1948), p. 131.

6 Hough, *Winston & Clementine*, p. 39.

7 Randolph S. Churchill, *Winston S. Churchill: Youth* (vol. 1) (London: Heinemann, 1966), p. 189.

8 James Leasor, *Rhodes and Barnato: The Premier and the Prancer* (Barnsley: Pen & Sword, 1996), p. 178.

9 Ted Morgan, *Churchill: The Rise to Failure, 1874–1915* (London: Triad Panther Books, 1984), p. 83.

10 Ibid., p. 85. Churchill later instituted proceedings against *Blackwood's Magazine*, which did not defend the case and placed a full apology.

11 *The Alyson Almanac* (New York: Alyson Publications), 1990, p. 107.

12 Ralph G. Martin, *Lady Randolph Churchill* (vol. 1) (London: Sphere Books, 1974), p. 44.

13 Haldane, *A Soldier's Saga*, p. 119.

14 Celia Sandys, *Churchill Wanted Dead or Alive* (London: Harper Collins, 1999), p. 16.

Chapter 2: Across the Great Karoo

1 Churchill, *London to Ladysmith via Pretoria* (London: Longmans Green, 1900), pp. 29–30.

2 Eric Bolsmann mentions Petrus Pretorius. See Bolsmann, *Winston*

Churchill: The Making of a Hero in the South African War (Alberton: Galago, 2008), p. 212.

3   George W. Stevens, *From Capetown to Ladysmith: An Unfinished Record of the South African War* (Edinburg and London: William Blackwood & Sons, 1900), pp. 1–2.

4   Lady Sarah Wilson, *South African Memories: Social, Warlike & Sporting. From Diaries Written at the Time* (London: Edward Arnold, 1909), p. 277.

5   Karel Schoeman, *Only an Anguish to Live Here: Olive Schreiner and the Anglo-Boer War 1899–1902* (Cape Town: Human & Rousseau, 1980), p. 200.

6   Raymond Sibbald, *The War Correspondents: The Boer War* (Johannesburg: Jonathan Ball, 1993), pp. 41–42.

7   Schoeman, *Only an Anguish to Live Here*, p. 200.

8   See Churchill, *London to Ladysmith via Pretoria*, Chapter 3.

9   Hough, *Winston & Clementine*, p. 111.

10 Brian Roberts, *Churchills in Africa* (London: Hamish Hamilton, 1970), p. 82.

11 Stevens, *From Capetown to Ladysmith*, pp. 12–13.

12 The local plumber in Beaufort West, C.A. Heyne, advertised in 1900 that he was extending his business and had imported machinery to 'bend iron for 50 to 400 gallon water tanks and to form single and double bend veranda roofs'. Among the bigger entrepreneurs were Bayer and Davidoff, general merchants, who opened a huge new store in Beaufort West in November 1901. They advertised an 'enormous stock', which included '2 350 pairs of boots and shoes, 2 800 shirts, 375 pairs of trousers, 150 suits, 300 dozen ties, 100 dresses, corsets from 2/6 to 15/-, 200 pieces of muslin, 50 pieces of silk, 50 different kinds of hats for gentlemen from 3/6 to 35/-, a huge variety of sailor hats for men, women and children – and, for a hot place like the Karoo – sunshades and umbrellas from 3/6d'. Bayer and Davidoff also stocked linoleums, carpets, tablecloths, curtains and groceries. Among their special opening offers was coffee at sixpence a pound. (From Karoo Rose/Rose Willis's stories mainly about the Karoo, page 10 capeinfo.com).

13 Capt. Stratford St Leger, *Boer War Sketches – Mounted Infantry at War* (Alberton: Galago Publishing, 1986), pp. 8–9.

14 Ibid., pp. 3–4.

15 Stevens, *From Capetown to Ladysmith*, p.10.

16 An interesting fact is that Molteno is the original home of the well-known South African rusks, Ouma Rusks. Simba was founded in Molteno in 1939, in a period of severe depression for the farming community. Anna Greyvenstein, the wife of a local farmer, was one of several women given a few shillings each by the church and encouraged to increase value in the best way possible in the interests of the community. She set about baking rusks – so successfully that it blossomed into the mighty business it is today. Packets of Ouma Rusks and Simba chips can be found in nearly every grocery store and café in the country. 'Ouma' died in 1988 in her late 90s.

Chapter 3: The green hills of Natal

1 Churchill, *London to Ladysmith via Pretoria*, pp. 53–54.

2 Ibid., pp. 39–40.

3 David Fordham and Pamela Todd, *Private Tucker's Boer War Diary* (London: Elm Tree Books, 1980), p. 22.

4 Churchill, *London to Ladysmith via Pretoria*, pp. 43–44.

5 Haldane, *A Soldier's Saga*, p. 138.

6 Sandys, *Churchill Wanted Dead or Alive*, p. 36.

7 Park Gray was later involved in the Battle of Colenso and the Relief of Ladysmith, and in 1906 served as an officer with the Natal Carbineers in the Zulu Rebellion. During the German South-West African campaign in World War I, he commanded the Natal Light Horse.

8 Robert Elliot Stevenson, 'A carbineer remembers', *Military History Journal* 2 (2), December 1971.

9 Hugh W. Kinsey, 'Churchill and Ladysmith', *Military History Journal* 7 (3), June 1987.

10 Churchill, *London to Ladysmith via Pretoria*, pp. 67–68.

Chapter 4: Captured by the Boers

1 Churchill, *My Early Life*, p. 249.

2 Haldane, *A Soldier's Saga*, p. 131.

3 Ibid., pp. 142–143.

4 Sir Frederick Treves, *The Tale of a Field Hospital* (London: Cassell & Company, 1900), p. 3.

5 Haldane, *A Soldier's Saga*, pp. 144–145. Ten years later, Wagner was decorated with the Albert Medal First Class on the recommendation of Churchill (then home secretary), while the train's second engineer, Alexander Stewart, received the same medal second class. Atkins, the correspondent from the *Manchester Guardian*, wrote that they had heard accounts saying that with bullets spattering around them, Churchill said, 'Keep cool, men.' And 'This will be interesting for my paper.' See Hugh Martin, *Battle: The Life Story of Winston Churchill* (London: Victor Gallancz, 1940), p. 43. The latter sounds unlikely, but the thought must have been uppermost in Churchill's mind.

6 Churchill, *My Early Life*, p. 249.

7 Kinsey, 'Churchill and Ladysmith'.

8 Sandys, *Churchill Wanted Dead or Alive*, p. 62. Churchill met General Botha's daughter, Helen, for the first time in 1907 at the Colonial Conference in London. There was gossip of a possible engagement between the two, but Helen denied many years later that there had ever been anything more than just friendship. 'It was so unlikely I would fall for him,' she said, stressing that after all she was 'a Transvaler'.

9 Randolph S. Churchill, *Winston S. Churchill: Youth* (vol. 1), p. 464.

10 Kenneth Griffith, *Thank God We Kept the Flag Flying: The Siege and Relief of Ladysmith, 1899–1900* (London: The Viking Press, 1975), p. 134.

11 C.J. Barnard, *Generaal Louis Botha op die Natalse Front, 1899–1900* (Cape Town: A.A. Balkema, 1970), p. 37.

12 Gail Nattrass and S.B. Spies, *Jan Smuts: Memoirs of the Boer War* (Cape Town: Jonathan Ball, 1994), p. 74.

13 Johannes Meintjies, *General Louis Botha: A Biography* (London: Cassell, 1970), p. 40.

14 Gen. Jan Kemp, *Vir Vryheid en vir Reg* (Cape Town: Nasionale Pers, 1941).

15 'Hagenaar nam Churchill in Zuid-Afrika gevangen', Amigoe di Curaçao, 19 January 1965, p. 5.

16 Haldane, *A Soldier's Saga*, p. 146.

17 Ibid., p. 142.

18 Fordham and Todd, *Private Tucker's Boer War Diary*, p. 38.

19 Gilbert, *Churchill: A Life*, pp. 19–20.

20 Bolsmann, *Winston Churchill: The Making of a Hero in the South African War*, p. 187.

Chapter 5: Prisoner of war in Pretoria

1 Churchill, *From London to Ladysmith via Pretoria*, pp. 108–109.

2 Churchill, *My Early Life*, p. 264.

3 Sandys, *Churchill Wanted Dead or Alive*, p. 72.

4 Churchill, *From London to Ladysmith via Pretoria*.

5 J.C. de Villiers, *Healers, Helpers and Hospitals*, Vols I & II (Pretoria: Protea Book House, 2008), p. 570.

6 The Staatsmodelschool was designed by the Dutch architect Sytze Wopke Wierda. A map following the course of the war, drawn by fellow prisoner Lieutenant T.H.C. Frankland during Churchill's captivity, is still displayed in the school building. Churchill described the Staatsmodelschool as a large, solid one-storey building, consisting of twelve large classrooms, seven or eight of which were used by the British officers as dormitories and one as a dining room. There was also a large lecture hall, which served as an improvised fives court, and a well-fitted gymnasium. The school stood in a quadrangular playground about 120 yards square, in which there were a dozen tents for the police guards, a cookhouse, two tents for the soldier servants, and a newly built shed for baths.

7 Hough, *Winston & Clementine*, p. 118.

8 Deneys Reitz, *Commando: A Boer Journal of the Boer War* (London: Faber & Faber, 1929), p. 49.

9 Randolph S. Churchill, *Winston S. Churchill: Youth*, pp. 479–480.

10 Ibid., p. 483.

11 Ibid., p. 484.

Chapter 6: Escape for Delagoa Bay

1 Churchill, *London to Ladysmith via Pretoria*, p. 190.

2 Ibid.

3 Ibid.

4 Haldane, *A Soldier's Saga*, pp. 167–168.

5 For the landlocked Transvaal, Delagoa Bay in the then Portuguese colony of Mozambique was its only link with the sea outside British control, the port of Lourenço Marques having been connected to Pretoria by rail on 8 July 1895 by means of the Eastern Line.

6 Churchill, *London to Ladysmith via Pretoria*, pp. 195–196.

7 Churchill, *My Early Life*, p. 281.

8 Churchill wrote: 'I then learned, to my surprise, that the mine was only about two hundred feet deep.' According to author Eric Bolsmann, it was only sixty feet deep. (Bolsmann, *Winston Churchill*, pp. 157–158.)

9 Churchill, *My Early Life*, p. 283.

10 On 14 December, one of the two Scottish miners, Mac, took Churchill around the old workings of the mine,

and near the bottom of the shaft they saw rats, which Churchill described as white, with dark eyes, which he was assured were bright pink in daylight. Three years afterwards, a British officer on duty in the district wrote to Churchill that he had heard his statement at a lecture about the white rats and their pink eyes, and thought it was the limit of 'mendacity'. He had then visited the mine to see for himself, and later apologised for having doubted Churchill's 'truthfulness'.

Chapter 7: Return to freedom

1 Churchill, *My Early Life*, p. 293.
2 Lodewijk Daniel de Haas was born in the Netherlands and initially served with the garrison division; he later served in Platoon III of the First Hollander Corps. De Haas was not involved in the Battle of Elandslaagte in October 1899, where the Hollander Corps suffered heavy casualties. De Haas later moved from the Transvaal to England.
3 The railway from Komatipoort to Pretoria reached Waterval Boven in March 1894. In order to establish a supply depot, the Transvaal Republic acquired about seventy-eight hectares of Doornhoek Farm, lying on either side of the line. Between Waterval Onder and Waterval Boven, the line rises from the Elands River valley and the Lowveld to the eastern edge of the Highveld – 208 metres over a distance of 7.5 kilometres, which necessitated a rack railway and a steep, curving tunnel over this stretch. This route was later changed to a less severe

gradient over a fourteen-kilometre stretch with two tunnels. After this diversion, the old tunnel was used for road traffic until 1936, when the Elands Pass was built. The original tunnel and the bridge just below the tunnel were proclaimed national monuments.
4 Franco Seiner, *Ervaringen en Herinneringen van Een Boerenstrijder* (Doesburg: J.C. van Schenk Brill, 1902), pp. 19–20.
5 This old Victorian building was built during the 1880s and used as the town hall from 1885 to 1910, until the town grew unexpectedly, and a newer, bigger town hall was needed. Before the arrival of skyscrapers, the post office and the new city hall were the most prominent features of Durban's horizon. It was also the venue in 1908 for negotiations to unify the four provinces of South Africa. It has been proclaimed a national monument.
6 West Street, leading through the centre of the city, is the principal street and was named after Lieutenant Governor of Natal Martin West (governor from 1845 to 1850).
7 Hough, *Winston & Clementine*, p. 124.
8 Ibid., p. 125.
9 Ibid., pp. 124–125.
10 Churchill-biased journalist Hugh Martin suggested that 'there was no deeply thought-out scheme. He just climbed the wall at night when the sentries had their back turned, and nobody else was quick enough to follow.' See Martin, *Battle: The Life Story of Winston Churchill*, p. 45.

Chapter 8: Colenso and Spioen Kop

1 Churchill, *London to Ladysmith via Pretoria*, pp. 306–307.
2 The original property in Longmarket Street had an unpretentious thatched cottage, but the years brought many changes; during the 1850s, it was transformed into a more substantial shale-built house, and further enlargements followed in the governorships of Keate (1868) and Havelock (1888), and in 1901 a red-brick wing was added. It became the Natal Training College in 1912, and today it provides offices for the staff of its successor institution, the Natal College of Education.
3 Fordham and Todd, *Private Tucker's Boer War Diary*, p. 40.
4 Hough, *Winston & Clementine*, p. 124.
5 Lieut. C.R.N. Burne, *With the Naval Brigade in Natal (1899–1900): Journal of Active Service kept During the Relief of Ladysmith and Subsequent Operations in Northern Natal and the Transvaal, under General Sir Redvers Buller, V.C., G.C.B.* (London: Edward Arnold, 1902), p. 22.
6 Hough, *Winston & Clementine*, p. 126.
7 'Nursing Notes', *The Nursing Record & Hospital World*, 10 February 1900, p. 114.
8 Sibbald, *The War Correspondents*, p. 56.
9 Churchill, *London to Ladysmith via Pretoria*, pp. 254–255.
10 Sandys, *Churchill Wanted Dead or Alive*, p. 152.
11 Gandhi believed that justice was on the side of the Boers, but that the Indians in South Africa had to seize the opportunity to show their loyalty to the British Empire in an effort to gain more political freedom. Therefore, he organised a volunteer ambulance corps to help the British during the first few months of the war. They served at several battlefields, including Colenso and Spioen Kop.

Chapter 9: Tugela Heights and the relief of Ladysmith

1 Churchill, *London to Ladysmith via Pretoria*, p. 339.
2 Ibid.
3 A. Wessels, *Die Militêre Rol van Swart Mense, Bruin Mense en Indiërs tydens die Anglo-Boereoorlog (1899–1902)* (Bloemfontein: Anglo-Boer War Museum, 1998), p. 8; P. Warwick (ed.), *The South African War: The Anglo-Boer War, 1899–1902* (Harlow: Longman, 1980), p. 201.
4 Sibbald, *The War Correspondents*, p.165.
5 A Central News report of 10 February in The Nursing Record & Hospital World mentions the arrival of an ambulance train with about a hundred wounded soldiers from the hospitals of Maritzburg bound for the hospital ship, the *Maine*. ('Nursing notes', *The Nursing Record & Hospital World*, p. 114.)
6 Churchill, *London to Ladysmith via Pretoria*.
7 Ibid, pp. 463–464.
8 'Eyewitness and personal accounts: Lionel James', www.ladysmithhistory.com. Accessed 3 June 2012.
9 Churchill, *My Early Life*, p. 325.
10 Richard Harding Davis, *With Both Armies in South Africa* (New York: Charles Scribner's Sons, 1901), pp. 74–75.
11 Ibid., pp. 85–86.

12 Churchill, *London to Ladysmith via Pretoria*, pp. 474–475.

13 Ibid.

Chapter 10: Free State journey

1 Churchill, *Ian Hamilton's March* (London: Longmans Green, 1900), p. 29.

2 Karel Schoeman, *Bloemfontein: Die Ontstaan van 'n Stad 1846–1946* (Cape Town: Human & Rousseau, 1980), p. 158.

3 William Edward Sellers, *From Aldershot to Pretoria: A Story of Christian Work Among Our Troops in South Africa* (London: The Religious Tract Society, 1900), p. 146.

4 Churchill, *Ian Hamilton's March*, pp. 6–9.

5 Ibid. pp. 10–14.

6 Ibid. pp. 16–17.

7 J.W. Milne, *Diary of No. 8080 Private J.W. Milne, 1st Service Company Volunteers, Gordon Highlanders (1900) During the Boer War*, www.jwmilne. freeservers.com. Accessed 29 July 2012.

8 E.A. Venter, *De Aar – Town of the Future (1902–1952)* (De Aar: De Aar Municipality), p. 11.

9 Lionel James (pseud. 'The Intelligence Officer'), *On the Heels of De Wet* (Edinburgh and London: William Blackwood & Sons, 1902), p. 2.

10 Hough, *Winston & Clementine*, p. 130.

11 J.W. Milne, *Diary of No. 8080 Private J.W. Milne*, www.jwmilne.freeservers. com.

12 Ibid.

13 Humphrey Carpenter (ed.), *The Letters of JRR Tolkien* (London: George Allen & Unwin, Houghton Mifflin, 1981), p. 213. Tolkien's father, Arthur, manager of the Bank of Africa, planted cypresses, pine trees and cedars at the bank premises. Arthur married Mabel Suffield on 16 April 1891 at Cape Town Cathedral, and two children – John Ronald Reuel (b. 1892) and Hilary Arthur Reuel (b. 1894) – were born from the marriage. The family lived next door to the bank. Mabel returned to England with the boys in 1895, but Arthur remained in Bloemfontein, where he died of rheumatic fever on 15 February 1896. He is buried in the President Brand Cemetery, on the corner of Church and Rhodes avenues in Bloemfontein.

Chapter 11: Towards the Transvaal

1 Churchill, *My Early Life*, p. 343.

2 Dewetsdorp, named after Jacobus Ignatius De Wet, father of General Christiaan de Wet, lies on the R702, seventy-five kilometres south-east of Bloemfontein. Most of the town's attractions and tourist sites relate to the struggle of the soldiers in the Anglo-Boer War. Jacobus de Wet was field cornet for this area, and campaigned for a village in the vicinity of Kareefontein Farm. An application was refused by the Volksraad in 1876, but De Wet and others bought Kareefontein and divided it into residential stands. In 1880 it was proclaimed a town under the name Dewetsdorp and became a municipality in 1890. During the war, the town was occupied by a British garrison after the fall of Bloemfontein, and on 19 November 1900 General Christiaan de Wet attacked the garrison under Major W.G. Massy, who surrendered four days later. The area is

prime sheep and cattle-ranching country, and the main crops are wheat and maize.

3   Churchill, *Ian Hamilton's March*, p. 56.

4   St Leger, *Boer War Sketches – Mounted Infantry at War*, pp. 107, 112.

5   Churchill, *Ian Hamilton's March*, pp. 159–162.

6   Ibid, p. 188.

7   Ken Gillings, 'Major Barr's pilgrimage: An old warrior revisits his Anglo-Boer War battlefields', *Military History Journal* 3 (3), June 1975.

8   Churchill, *Ian Hamilton's March*, pp. 200–201.

9   Ibid, pp. 201–204.

10 Ibid., p. 217.

11 Karel Schoeman, *Vrystaatse Erfenis* (Cape Town: Human & Rousseau, 1982), p. 124.

12 Sibbald, *The War Correspondents*, p. 187.

13 'Boere-oorlog stories: Heilbron en omgewing', *Heilbron Herald*, 2006.

14 The Caledonian Hotel burnt down in 1912 and was restored as the Commercial Hotel, which is still there today, although not in its original state after restoration.

15 Churchill, *Ian Hamilton's March*, p. 230.

Chapter 12: Cycling through Johannesburg

1   Churchill, *Ian Hamilton's March*, p. 238.

2   Gillings, 'Major Barr's Pilgrimage'.

3   Churchill, *Ian Hamilton's March*, p. 271.

4   Wilson, *South African Memories: Social, Warlike & Sporting From Diaries Written at the Time* (London: Edward Arnold, 1909), p. 42.

Chapter 13: The fall of Pretoria

1   Churchill, *Ian Hamilton's March*, pp. 291–292.

2   Sibbald, *The War Correspondents*, p. 191.

3   Frederick Maurice Crum, *With the Mounted Infantry in South Africa* (Cambridge: McMilland & Bowes, 1903), pp. 61–62.

4   Seiner, *Ervaringen en Herinneringen van Een Boerenstrijder*, p. 25. Translated by the author.

5   Wilson, *South African Memories*, pp. 44–45.

6   Ibid., pp. 234–235.

7   Ibid., p. 237.

8   Ibid., pp. 239–240.

9   Hough, *Winston & Clementine*, p. 131.

10 Sibbald, *The War Correspondents*, p. 200.

Bibliography

Books

Amery, Leo S. (ed.). *The Times History of the War in South Africa*. London: Sampson Low, Marston & Company, 1905

Atkins, J.B. *Incidents and Reflections*. London: Christopher's, 1947

———. *The Relief of Ladysmith*. London: Methuen, 1900

Balsan, Consuelo V. *The Glitter and the Gold*. New York: George Mann, 1973

Barnard, C.J. *Generaal Louis Botha op die Natalse Front, 1899–1900*. Cape Town: A.A. Balkema, 1970

Baynes, Right Rev. Arthur Hamilton. *My Diocese During the War – Extracts from the Diary of the Right Reverend Arthur Hamilton Baynes, D.D., Bishop of Natal*. London: George Bell, 1900

Bolsmann, Eric. *Winston Churchill: The Making of a Hero in the South African War*. Alberton: Galago, 2008

Botes, Paul. *History of Witbank*. Witbank: Witbank City Council, 1994

Breytenbach, J.H. *Die Geskiedenis van die Tweede Vryheidsoorlog in Suid-Afrika 1899–1902* (in five volumes). Cape Town: Government Printers, 1996

Burne, Lieut. Charles Richard Newdigate. *With the Naval Brigade in Natal (1899–1900): Journal of Active Service Kept During the Relief of Ladysmith and Subsequent Operations in Northern Natal and the Transvaal, Under General Sir Redvers Buller, V.C., G.C.B.* London: Edward Arnold, 1902

Carpenter, Humphrey (ed.). *The Letters of JRR Tolkien*. London: George Allen & Unwin, Houghton Mifflin, 1981

Childs, Lewis. *Ladysmith: The Siege*. Barnsley: Leo Cooper, 1999

Churchill, Lady Randolph: *The Reminiscences of Lady Randolph Churchill*. New York: Century, 1908

Churchill, Randolph S. *Winston S. Churchill: Youth* (vol. 1). London: Heinemann, 1966

Churchill, Sir Winston. *Ian Hamilton's March*. London: Longmans Green, 1900

———. *London to Ladysmith via Pretoria*. London: Longmans Green, 1900

———. *Lord Randolph Churchill*. London: Macmillan, 1906

———. *My Early Life*. London: Thornton Butterworth, 1930

————. *The River War*. London: Longmans Green, 1899, 1900

————. *The Story of the Malakand Field Force*. London: Longmans Green, 1898

Cilliers, Johannes Hermanus. *Die Slag van Spioenkop 24 Januarie 1900*. Archives Yearbook for SA History 1960, Part II

Colenso Town Borough. *The Battle of Colenso, 15th December 1899*. Colenso: Colenso Town Borough (no date)

Conan Doyle, Arthur. *The Great Boer War*. London: Smith, Elder & Co., 1902

Cowles, Virginia. *Winston Churchill: The Era and the Man*. New York: Grosset & Dunlap, 1953

Crum, Frederick Maurice. *With the Mounted Infantry in South Africa*. Cambridge: McMilland & Bowes, 1903

Davis, Richard Harding. *With Both Armies in South Africa*. New York: Charles Scribner's Sons, 1901

De Jong, R.C., G.M. Van der Waal and D.H. Heydenrych. *NZASM 100: 1887–1899, the buildings, steam engines and structures of the Netherlands South African Railway Company*. Pretoria: C. van Rensburg Publications on behalf of the Human Sciences Research Council, 1988

De Villiers, J.C. *Healers, Helpers and Hospitals*, Vols I & II. Pretoria: Protea Book House, 2008

Erasmus, D.F. *Heilbron 1873–1973 – Feesalbum*. Heilbron: Stadsraad van Heilbron, 1973

Fordham, David, and Pamela Todd. *Private Tucker's Boer War Diary*. London: Elm Tree Books, 1980

Gilbert, Martin. *Churchill: A Life*. London: Pimlico, 2000

————. *Churchill: A Photographic Portrait*. London: Heinemann, 1974

Greaves, Allan. *Tell Me of Komani … A History of Queenstown*. Queenstown: Queenstown and Frontier Historical Society, 1987

Griffith, Kenneth. *Thank God We Kept the Flag Flying: The Siege and Relief of Ladysmith, 1899–1900*. London: The Viking Press, 1974

Guedalla, Philip. *Mr Churchill: A Portrait*. London: Hodder & Stoughton, 1941

Haldane, Aylmer. *A Soldier's Saga*. Edinburgh and London: William Blackwood & Sons, 1948

————. *How We Escaped from Pretoria*. Edinburgh and London: William Blackwood & Sons, 1900

Hall, Darrell. *Halt! Action! Front! With Colonel Long at Colenso*. Weltevreden Park: Covos-Day Books, 1994

Hamilton, Sir Ian. *Listening for the Drums*. London: Faber & Faber, 1944

A Handbook of the Boer War. London and Aldershot: Butler & Tanner, 1910

Heath, Isak S. *Die Rooi Bul van Krugersdorp: Veggeneraal S.F. Oosthuizen: Sy Aandeel in die Verloop van die Anglo-Boere-Oorlog 1899–1900*. Centurion: Isak Heath, 1999

———. *The Man who Captured Churchill*. Centurion: Isak Heath, 2000

Heilbron Herald. 'Boere-Oorlog Stories: Heilbron en Omgewing'. *Heilbron: Heilbron Herald*, 2006

Horton, Alice. *Kruger's Secret Service, By One Who Was In It*. London: John Macqueen, 1900

Hough, Richard. *Winston & Clementine: The Triumph of the Churchills*. London: Bantam, 1990

Hurst, H.H. *Winston Churchill: War Correspondent, South African War*. Durban: Knox, 1944

James, Lionel (pseud. 'The Intelligence Officer'). *On the Heels of De Wet*. Edinburgh and London: William Blackwood & Sons, 1902

Jeans, Thomas T. *Naval Brigades in the South African War, 1899–1900*. London: Sampson, Low, Marston & Co, 1900

Jenkins, Roy. *Churchill: A Biography*. London: Macmillan, 2001

Johannesburg 100 Years. Johannesburg: Chris van Niekerk Publications, 1986

Kemp, Gen. Jan. *Vir Vryheid en Reg*. Cape Town: Nasionale Pers, 1941

Kepper, George Lodewijk. *De Zuid-Afrikaansche Oorlog: Historisch Gedenkboek*. Leiden: Sijthoff, circa 1903

Laband, John, and Rob Haswell (eds.). *Pietermaritzburg 1838–1988: A New Portrait of an African City*. Pietermaritzburg: University of Natal Press and Shuter & Shuter, 1988

Leasor, James. *Rhodes and Barnato: The Premier and the Prancer*. Barnsley: Pen & Sword, 1996

Lee, Emanoel. *To the Bitter End: A Photographic History of the Boer War, 1899–1902*. Harmondsworth: Penguin, 1985

Malan, André. *Oorwinning sonder Roem. 'n Foto-album van herinnerings aan die Anglo-Boereoorlog 1899–1902*. Pretoria: J.P. van der Walt, 1999

Manchester, William. *The Last Lion: Winston Spencer Churchill: Visions of Glory, 1874–1932*. New York: Little, Brown & Company, 1983

Martin, Hugh. *Battle: The Life Story of Winston Churchill*. London: Victor Gallancz, 1940

Martin, Ralph G. *Lady Randolph Churchill* (vol. 1). London: Sphere Books, 1974

McLachlan, Jimmy L. *My Time and Churchill's Eight Watches* (compiled by J.A. McLachlan). Pretoria (no date)

Meintjies, Johannes. *General Louis Botha: A Biography*. London: Cassell, 1970

———. *Stormberg, a Lost Opportunity: The Anglo-Boer War in the North-Eastern Cape Colony, 1899–1902*. Cape Town: Nasionale Boekhandel, 1969

Morgan, Ted. *Churchill: The Rise to Failure 1874–1915*. London: Triad Panther Books, 1984

Nattrass, Gail, and S.B. Spies. *Jan Smuts: Memoirs of the Boer War*. Cape Town: Jonathan Ball, 1994

Oosthuizen, Abrie V. *A Guide to the Battlefields, Graves and Monuments of the Anglo-Boer War in the North Eastern Cape: Hundredth Anniversary, 1899–1999*. Bloemfontein: War Museum of the Boer Republics, 1998

Pakenham, Thomas. *The Boer War*. New York: Avon Books, 1979

Penning, Louwrens. *De Oorlog in Zuid-Afrika*. Three Volumes. Rotterdam: D.A. Daamen, 1902

Phillips, Lisle March. *With Rimington*. London: Edward Arnold, 1902

Playne, Somerset. *Cape Colony: Its History, Commerce, Industries & Resources*. Cape Town: Juta & Co., 1910

Reckitt, B.N. *The Lindley Affair: A Diary of the Boer War*. Hull: A. Brown & Sons, 1972

Reitz, Deneys. *Commando: A Boer Journal of the Boer War*. London: Faber & Faber, 1929

Roberts, Brian. *Churchills in Africa*. London: Hamish Hamilton, 1970

———. *Those Bloody Women: Three Heroines of the Boer War*. London: John Murray, 1991

St Leger, Capt. Stratford. *Boer War Sketches – Mounted Infantry at War*. Alberton: Galago, 1986

Sandberg, Dr C.G.S. *De Zesdaagse Slag aan de Boven Tugela*. Amsterdam: G.H. Priem, 1900

Sandys, Celia. *Churchill Wanted Dead or Alive*. London: Harper Collins, 1999

Schoeman, Chris. *Brothers in Arms: Hollanders in the Anglo-Boer War 1899–1902*. Cape Town: Zebra Press, 2011

Schoeman, Karel. *Bloemfontein: Die Ontstaan van 'n Stad 1846–1946*. Cape Town: Human & Rousseau, 1980

———. *Only an Anguish to Live Here: Olive Schreiner and the Anglo-Boer War, 1899–1902*. Cape Town: Human & Rousseau, 1980

———. *Vrystaatse Erfenis*. Cape Town: Human & Rousseau, 1982

Scott, Dot. *Girl in a Blue Bonnet: The True Story of a Woman's Quest in Africa*. Pretoria: Crink, 2008

Seiner, Franco. *Ervaringen en Herinneringen van Een Boerenstrijder*. Doesburg: J.C. van Schenk Brill, 1902

Sellers, William Edward. *From Aldershot to Pretoria: A Story of Christian Work among Our Troops in South Africa*. London: The Religious Tract Society, 1900

Sibbald, Raymond. *The War Correspondents: The Boer War.* Johannesburg: Jonathan Ball, 1993

Slegtkamp, Henri Frederick. *Slegtkamp van Spioenkop: Oorlogsherinneringe van Kapt. Slegtkamp.* Compiled from his diary by Dirk Mostert. Cape Town: Nasionale Pers, 1935

Smail, J.L. *Those Restless Years.* Cape Town: Howard Timmins, 1971

Smurthwaite, David. *The Boer War 1899–1902.* London: Hamlyn, 1999

Stevens, George W. *From Capetown to Ladysmith: An Unfinished Record of the South African War.* Edinburg and London: William Blackwood & Sons, 1900

Sykes, Lady Jessica. *Side Lights on the War in South Africa (1900).* Whitefish: Kessinger Publishing, 2009

Taitz, Jerold (ed.). *The War Memoirs of Commandant Ludwig Krause 1899–1900.* Cape Town: Van Riebeeck Society, 1996

The Alyson Almanac. New York: Alyson Publications, 1990

Theron, Bridget. *Pretoria at War 1899–1900.* Pretoria: Protea Book House, 2000

Treves, Sir Frederick. *The Tale of a Field Hospital.* London: Cassell & Company, 1900

Van Winter, Pieter J. *Onder Krugers Hollanders: Geschiedenis van de Nederlandsche Zuid-Afrikaansche Spoorweg-Maatschappij.* Amsterdam: De Bussy, 1938

Venter, I.S.J. *Die Sendingstasie Tbaba Nchu 1833–1900.* Pretoria: Unisa, 1960

Viljoen, Ben. *Mijne Herinneringen uit den Anglo-Boeren-Oorlog.* Amsterdam: Versluys, 1902

Wallace, Edgar. *Unofficial Dispatches of the Anglo-Boer War.* 2nd edition. Cape Town: Struik, 1975

Warwick, P. (ed.). *The South African War: The Anglo-Boer War, 1899–1902.* Harlow: Longman, 1980

Watson, Abrie, and John Pretorius. *Boereoorlogstories van Heilbron: Verhale oor die Anglo-Boereoorlog van 1899–1902.* Heilbron: *Heilbron Herald*, 1999

Wessels, A. *Die Militêre Rol van Swart Mense, Bruin Mense en Indiërs tydens die Anglo-Boereoorlog (1899–1902).* Bloemfontein: Anglo-Boer War Museum, 1998

Williams, Sir Ralph. *How I Became a Governor.* London: John Murray, 1913

Wilson, Lady Sarah. *South African Memories: Social, Warlike & Sporting. From Diaries Written at the Time.* London: Edward Arnold, 1909

Woods, Frederick (ed.). *Young Winston's Wars.* London: Leo Cooper, 1972

Magazine and newspaper articles

Alexander, D. 'Winston Churchill once walked Pietermaritzburg's streets', *The Witness*, 8 April 1999

Fourie, Felicia. 'Four exceptional women in the Anglo-Boer War', *The South African Military History Society*, Smuts House Centenary Talk, 18 August 2009

Gillings, Ken. 'After the siege: The British advance and Boer retreat through Natal, March to June 1900', *Military History Journal* 11 (3/4), October 1999

————. 'Major Barr's pilgrimage: An old warrior revisits his Anglo-Boer War battlefields', *Military History Journal* 3 (3), June 1975

'Hagenaar nam Churchill in Zuid-Afrika gevangen', *Amigoe di Curaçao*, 19 January 1965

Kinsey, Hugh W. 'Churchill and Ladysmith', *Military History Journal* 7 (3), June 1987

Knox, R. 'Poor little rich girl', Tribune Magazine, 15 May 1953

Maurice, Sir Frederick. 'Mr Churchill as a military historian', *Foreign Affairs*, July 1927

————. 'The world crisis, 1916–1918', *Foreign Affairs*, 1927

'Nursing notes', *The Nursing Record & Hospital World*, 10 February 1900

Stevenson, Robert Elliot. 'A carbineer remembers', *Military History Journal* 2 (2), December 1971

The Standard Diggers' News, 14, 24 and 25 December 1899

The Star, 11 and 22 December 1923

Van Bart, Martiens. 'Winston Churchill was in SA géén oorlogsheld', *Die Burger*, 26 November 2011

Van der Walt, Sarel. 'Churchill se kroeg en die manne van die myn', *Die Burger*, 12 November 2010

Watt, Steve A. 'The Battle of Vaalkrans', *Military History Journal* 7 (2), December 1986

Electronic sources

Diary of a Boer War Veteran. 'Diary of No. 8080 Private J.W. Milne, 1st Service Company Volunteers, Gordon Highlanders (1900) during the Boer War', www.jwmilne.freeservers.com

Ladysmith History & the Boer War. 'Eyewitness and personal accounts: Lionel James', www.ladysmithhistory.com

TIME. www.time.com/time

Witbank – Mining-related Postcards. www.on-the-rand.co.uk/coalfields/witbank.htm

Picture sources

7: Manchester, *The Last Lion*
8: Gilbert, *Churchill: A Photographic Portrait*
11: Gilbert, *Churchill: A Photographic Portrait*
12: Gilbert, *Churchill: A Photographic Portrait*
13: http://www.woolworthsmuseum.co.uk
14: Manchester, *The Last Lion*
15: www.soldiersofthequeen.com
16: Allen, *Kruger's Pretoria*
17: Meintjies, *Die Anglo-Boereoorlog in Beeld*
18: Meintjies, *Die Anglo-Boereoorlog in Beeld*
21: Wilson, *South African Memories*
22: Smurthwaite, *The Boer War 1899–1902*
23: Author
24: Author's collection
25: Author's collection
26: Cape Archives
27: www.heritage-history.com
29: Author
31: www.probertencyclopaedia.com
32: Author
33 (**top**): Author's collection;
   (**middle and bottom**): Author
34: Schoeman, *Witnesses to War*
35: *Handbook of the Boer War*
36: Meintjies, *Die Anglo-Boereoorlog in Beeld*
37 (**top, middle and bottom**): Author
39 (**top and bottom**): Meintjies, *Stormberg,
   a Lost Opportunity*
40 (**top**): Meintjies, *Dorp van Drome*;
   (**bottom**): Playne, *Cape Colony*
41: Author
43: Author's collection
44: Author
45: Author's collection
46 (**top and bottom**): Author
48 (**top and bottom**): Author

49 (**top**): Author's collection;
   (**bottom**): Schoeman, *Witnesses to War*
50: *Handbook of the Boer War*
51: Pakenham, *The Boer War*
52: Sandys, *Churchill: Wanted Dead or Alive*
53: SA Military History Society
55: Author
56 (**top and bottom**): Author
58: Hall, *Halt! Action Front!*
59 (**top**): Haldane, *A Soldier's Saga*;
   (**bottom**): Smurthwaite, *The Boer War*
60: Fordham, *Private Tucker's Diary*
61: Author
62: www.geheugenvannederland.nl
63: Sandys, *Churchill: Wanted Dead or Alive*
66: Meintjies, *General Louis Botha*
67: Malan, *Ons Boere-offisiere*
71: Author
73: Lee, *To the Bitter End*
75: www.geheugenvannederland.nl
77: Kepper, *De Zuid-Afrikaansche Oorlog*
78: Sandys, *Churchill: Wanted Dead or Alive*
80: Sandys, *Churchill: Wanted Dead or Alive*
81: www.geheugenvannederland.nl
82: Sandys, *Churchill: Wanted Dead or Alive*
85: Spies and Natttrass, *Jan Smuts*
88: *Handbook of the Boer War*
91: www.geheugenvannederland.nl
93: Sandys, *Churchill: Wanted Dead or Alive*
94: Sandys, *Churchill: Wanted Dead or Alive*
95: Sandys, *Churchill: Wanted Dead or Alive*
97: Meintjies, *Die Anglo-Boereoorlog in Beeld*
100: Van Winter, *Onder Krugers Hollanders*
101 (**top**): De Jong, et al, *NZASM 100*;
   (**bottom**): www.geheugenvannederland.nl
102: De Jong, et al, *NZASM 100*

103: De Jong, et al, *NZASM 100*

104: www.geheugenvannederland.nl

105: Meintjies, *Die Anglo-Boereoorlog in Beeld*

106: Sandys, *Churchill: Wanted Dead or Alive*

107: Author

109: Oberholzer, *Die Historiese Monumente van SA*

110: *Handbook of the Boer War*

111: Vallentin, *Der Burenkrieg*

112 (**top**): Gilbert, *Churchill: A Photographic Portrait*; (**bottom**): Sandys, *Churchill: Wanted Dead or Alive*

113: *Handbook of the Boer War*

114: Smurthwaite, *The Boer War 1899–1902*

115: Author

116: Author

117: Malan, *Oorwinning sonder Roem*

118: Sandys, *Churchill: Wanted Dead or Alive*

119: Author

120: *Handbook of the Boer War*

121: Vallentin, *Der Burenkrieg*

122: Lee, *To the Bitter End*

123 (**top**): Meintjies, *Die Anglo-Boereoorlog in Beeld*; (**bottom**): Author

124/5: Author

126: Lee, *To the Bitter End*

127: www.wallpaperswala.com

129: Smurthwaite, *The Boer War 1899–1902*

130: http://commons.wikimedia.org/

131: Fordham, *Private Tucker's Diary*

132: Author

133: Author

134: *Handbook of the Boer War*

135 (**top**): www.geheugenvannederland.nl; (**bottom**): Author

136: Author

137: jssgallery.org

138: Smurthwaite, *The Boer War 1899–1902*

139: Smurthwaite, *The Boer War 1899–1902*

141: Vallentin, *Der Burenkrieg*

143: The Durban Club

144: Meintjies, *Die Anglo-Boereoorlog in Beeld*

145: Meintjies, *Die Anglo-Boereoorlog in Beeld*

146 (**top and bottom**): Schoeman, *Bloemfontein*

148: Schoeman, *Bloemfontein*

150: *Handbook of the Boer War*

152 (**top**): Grootfontein Agricultural Institute; (**bottom**): Author

153: reocities.com

154 (**top**): nuwegeskiedenis.co.za; (**bottom**): Anglo Boer War Museum

155: Durbach, *Kipling's South Africa*

157 (**top and bottom**): Author

159: Schoeman, *Vrystaatse Erfenis*

160: Anglo-Boer War Museum

161: Smurthwaite, *The Boer War 1899–1902*

162: Vallentin, *Der Burenkrieg*

163 (**top**): De Wet, *De Strijd tussen Boer en Brit*; (**bottom**): Vallentin, *Der Burenkrieg*

164: www.telegraph.co.uk

165: Author

167: Lee, *To the Bitter End*

170: Meintjies, *Die Anglo-Boereoorlog in Beeld*

171: Smurthwaite, *The Boer War 1899–1902*

172 (**top and bottom**): Author

174 (**top**): Schoeman, *Vrystaatse Erfenis*; (**bottom**): Author

175: Schoeman, *Vrystaatse Erfenis*

176: Erasmus, *Heilbron*

177: Schoeman, *Vrystaatse Erfenis*

179: Meintjies, *Die Anglo-Boereoorlog in Beeld*

180: *Handbook of the Boer War*

181: Meintjies, *Die Anglo-Boereoorlog in Beeld*

182: Kepper, *De Zuid-Afrikaansche Oorlog*

184: www.geheugenvannederland.nl

185: Meintjies, *Die Anglo-Boereoorlog in Beeld*

186: *Johannesburg 100 Years*

188: Allen, *Kruger's Pretoria*

189: Allen, *Kruger's Pretoria*

190: www.geheugenvannederland.nl

191: Meintjies, *Die Anglo-Boereoorlog in Beeld*

192: Meintjies, *Die Anglo-Boereoorlog in Beeld*

193: Meintjies, *Die Anglo-Boereoorlog in Beeld*

198: Meintjies, *Die Anglo-Boereoorlog in Beeld*

199: www.geheugenvannederland.nl

200: Anglo-Boer War Museum

201 (**top and bottom**): Author

202: www.zeevgalili.com

203: Bombled, *Les Boers*

205: *Reader's Digest Illustrated History of South Africa*

Index

Photographs, maps and illustrations are indicated by **bold** type.

Do you have any comments, suggestions or
feedback about this book or any other Zebra Press titles?
Contact us at talkback@zebrapress.co.za

*

Visit www.randomstruik.co.za and subscribe
to our newsletter for monthly updates and news

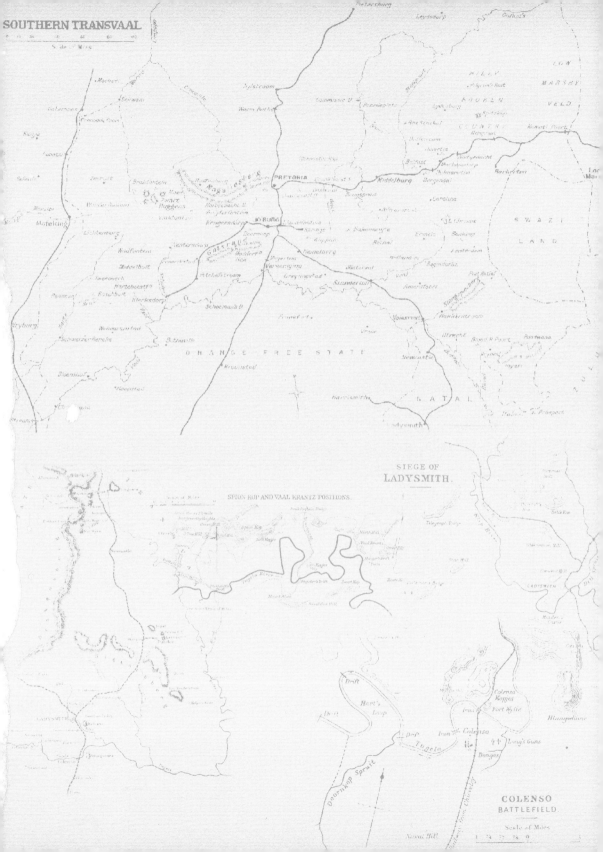

SOUTHERN TRANSVAAL

Scale of Miles

SIEGE OF
LADYSMITH.

SPION KOP AND VAAL KRANTZ POSITIONS.

COLENSO
BATTLEFIELD.

Scale of Miles

TRANSVAAL

BLOEMFONTEIN

B A S U T O L A N D

ORANGE FREE STATE

Scale of Miles

N A T A L

Ladysmith

ORANGE RIVER

DONKER POORT
OLIVE
AMASANGO
COLESBERG
PORT
KLEE PLAATS
ALIWAL NORTH
TEULTATANG
PLEW PAN
VENTERSTAD
AMPOAAR
ARENSBURG
BRANDSPRUIT
ARUNDEL
ALBERT J
BURGHERSDORP
TWEEDALE
NAUUWPOORT
ZOUR BERG M.
JAMESTOWN
RAYNER
STORMBERG M.
BOSWORTH
KROMHOOGTE
HENNING
STORMBERG J.
ROODE BERG
STEYNSBURG
CONTAT
ONVERWACHT
DORDRECHT
SHERBORNE
LOYANI
MOLTENO
BANGOR
THEBUS
SCHOMBIE
CYPHERGAT
ALANDALE
ROSMEAD
STERKSTROOM
MIDDLEBURG
TAFELBERG
MARAISBURG
PUTTERS KRAAL
SNEEUW
BERG
ROODE HOOGTE
BAILEY
LADY FRERE
PAARDE KRAAL
LESSEGTON
BETHESDA
ABODA
TARKASTAD
QUEENSTOWN
GLEN HARRY
KEI RIVER

Olifants R.

Cape Town   Worcester